AN EASY COURSE IN USING THE HP–12C

and other HP financial calculators

By Chris Coffin and Ted Wadman
Illustrated by Robert Bloch

Grapevine Publications, Inc.
P.O. Box 118
Corvallis, Oregon 97339–0118

We extend our thanks to Hewlett–Packard Company for producing such top–quality products and documentation.

Printed in the United States of America
7th Printing –– 1987

ISBN 0–931011–08–6

Read this first!

Time is an investment. If you spend it wisely, it will provide ENORMOUS RETURNS.

Invest your time in this book. It covers exactly what you need to know to use your HP financial calculator effectively. And you'll be learning to use it as quickly as you can. Remember, if you have time to use it, you have time to learn it first.

This book was written just for you. It lets you work at your own pace, so just relax, sit back and let the directions show you the way.

In this book, you will encounter many common applications in lending and investment analysis.

Yet as you read, it's a good idea to keep in mind that what you want to get out of this book is more than just this handful of specific keystroke procedures. You'll want to understand the fundamental principles involved. If you do this, then when you encounter a calculation you've never seen before (and maybe nobody else has either), you can confidently come up with the correct new solution. That skill is an asset valued by anyone and any business.

Now, grab your calculator...

This course can be used to learn about financial problem–solving on several HP calculators other than the HP–12C, such as the HP–37, HP–38, HP–67/97 (with pac software), and the HP–41 (with module software). If you want to learn with one of these other machines, then turn right now to page 248.

INTRODUCTION

HOW TO PICTURE IT

To begin, you have to be able to visualize what's going on inside the HP–12C. The next 8 pages paint a visual picture of the insides of your calculator. Set your calculator down now, and read and absorb the ideas until you are instructed to start pressing keys.

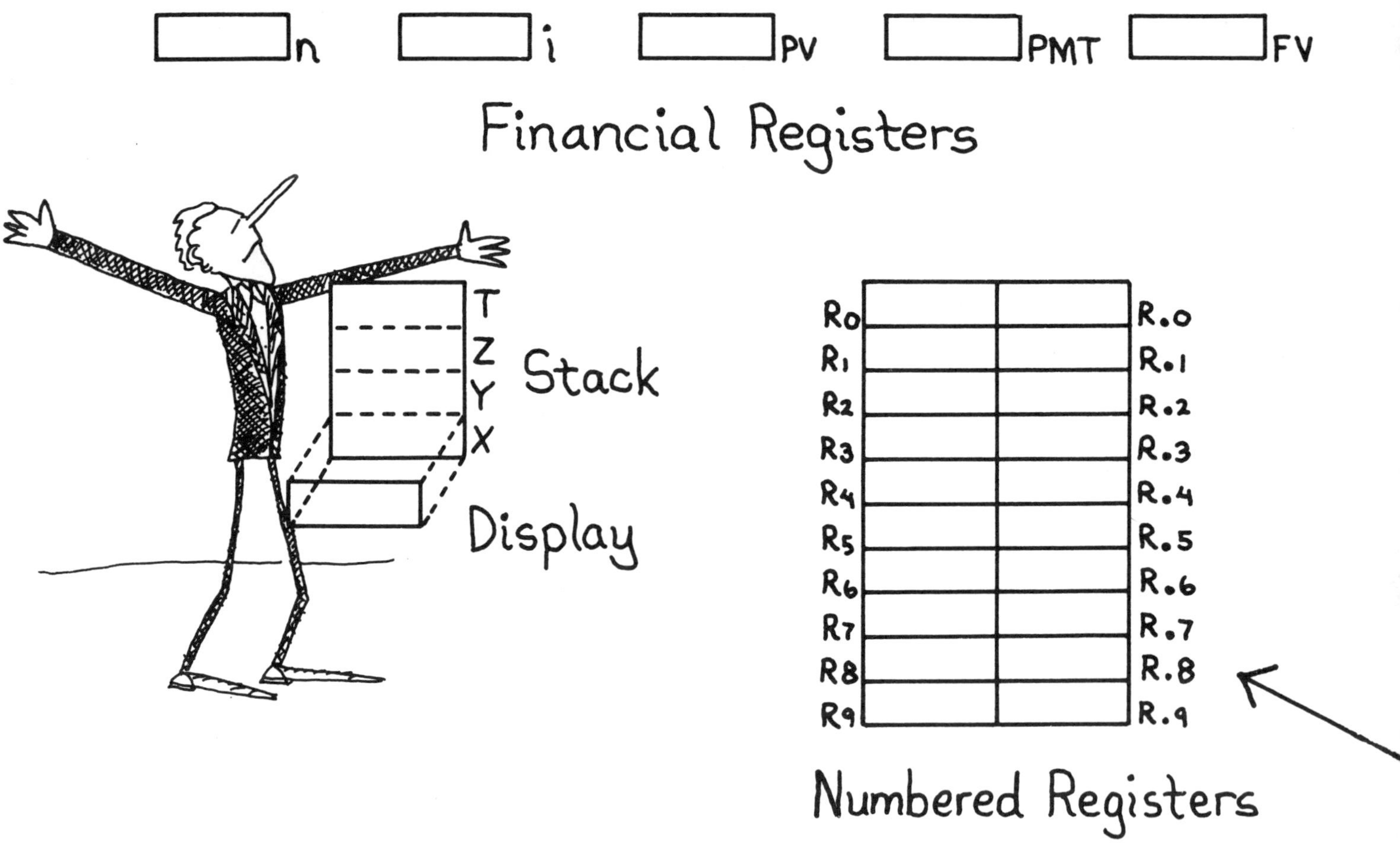

(If this is all unnecessary review, turn to page 14.)

Take a look at that last picture.

Each one of those boxes represents a storage register in the calculator.

"Right.... What's a storage register?"

A storage register is simply a place in the calculator's memory where it can store one number, and each such register has a name.

THE NUMBERED REGISTERS

Look first at this group of twenty storage registers here. Each of these registers is "named" with a number from 0 to 9 or .0 to .9.

You'll always use the "number–names" of these registers when you're using them for storage.

THE FINANCIAL REGISTERS

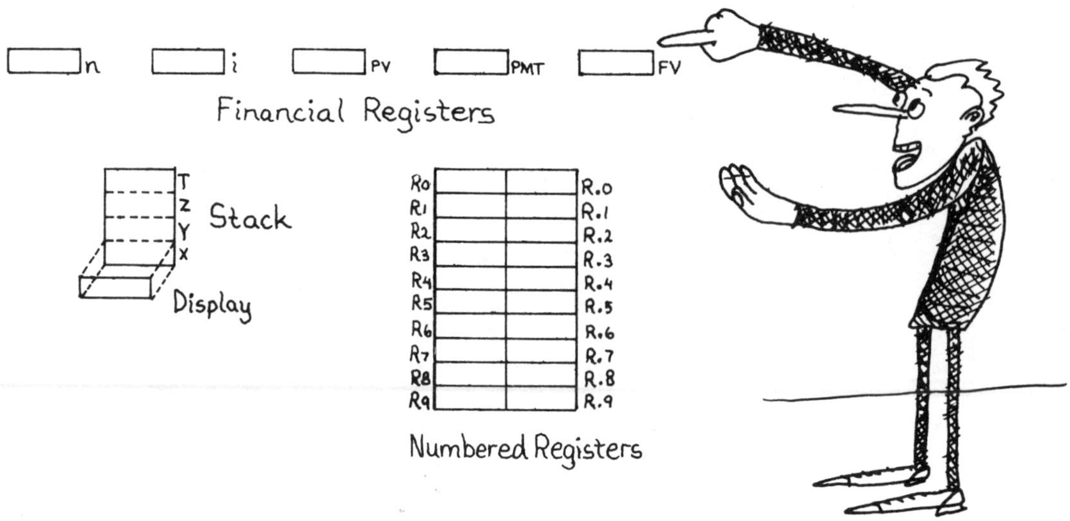

Next, notice the five financial registers:

[n] "number of periods"
[i] "interest rate"
[PV] "Present Value"
[PMT] "PayMenT"
[FV] "Future Value"

Just like any other storage registers, each of these will hold one number at a time, but the numbers stored in these registers mean something particular to your calculator. They're used in performing the financial calculations (financial calculators are designed to do financial calculations).

To do a financial calculation, you'll be directing your calculator to find one of those five numbers, and it will do so by using the other four.

THE STACK

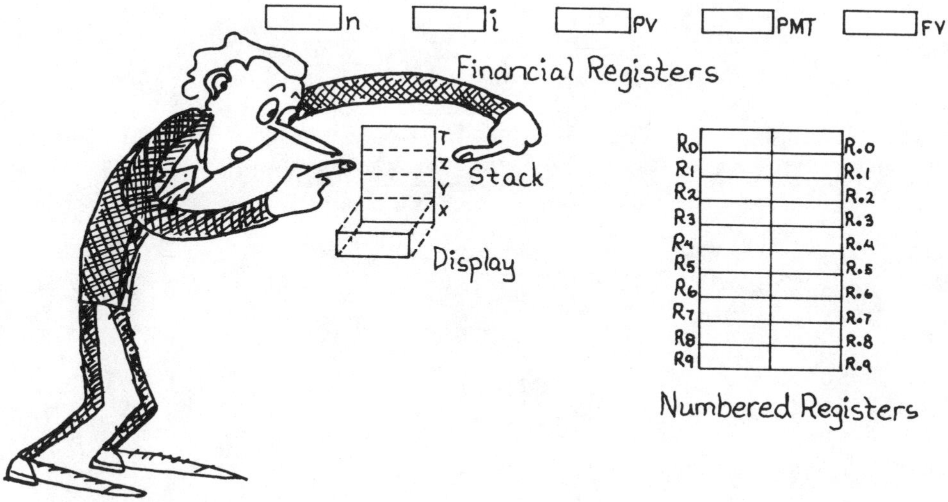

Look at the stack registers for a moment. Again, each of these four registers will hold one number at a time. But these registers are linked together in a certain way that makes them behave as if they're "stacked" on top of one another.

To help you remember this link between these registers, they're named X, Y, Z, and T (the T stands for "Top of the stack").

In many ways, the stack registers are the most important registers in the calculator, because most arithmetic is done there.

THE DISPLAY

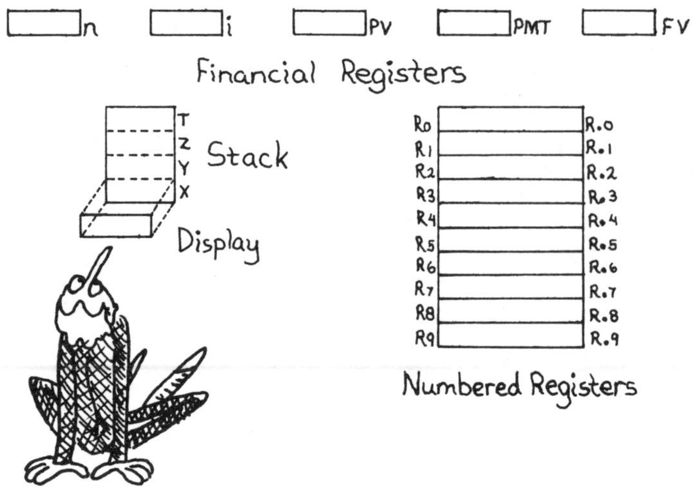

Now, notice the DISPLAY. It's shown here positioned over the X–register. The DISPLAY is ALWAYS positioned over the X–register (the bottom register of the stack).

The DISPLAY is the window of your calculator. It's what you look through to "see into" the machine.

WHEN YOU LOOK AT THE NUMBER IN THE DISPLAY, YOU ARE LOOKING AT THE NUMBER IN THE X–REGISTER, ALWAYS.

"But wait a minute...why should I bother thinking about the display as a window if it's always showing the X–register? Why not just think about the X–register?"

BECAUSE THE DISPLAY IS VERY DIFFERENT FROM THE X–REGISTER!

The display is really a separate "window." Sometimes it's partly shut; that is, it doesn't always show you the entirety of the number in the X–register.

In fact, the display will show you only as much of that number as you tell it to. The rest will be cut off, and the display will round the last digit.

You've read a lot of information in these pages. Here's a quick review to make sure that you're an expert on the concepts covered so far....

QUICK REVIEW

You should be able to answer these questions with no problem. The answers are on the next page. So go over any fuzzy areas NOW, before you go on.

1. What's a storage register?

2. How many numbers can one storage register hold at one time?

3. Name three different kinds of storage registers.

4. What is the display? How should you picture it?

5. Why is the stack named such?

6. How many registers are in the stack, and how are they named?

7. How many financial registers are there, and how are they named?

8. How many numbered registers are there, and how are they named?

QUICK ANSWERS

1. A storage register is the place where the calculator stores numbers (see page 8).

2. Only one number at a time can be stored in a storage register (page 8).

3. Three types of storage registers are: NUMBERED registers, FINANCIAL registers, and the STACK registers (page 7).

4. The display is like a window that always shows part or all of the number in the X–register (pages 11 and 12).

5. The stack is so named because these registers are linked together in a way that resembles a stack––to allow arithmetic (page 10).

6. There are four STACK registers, named X, Y, Z, T.

7. There are five FINANCIAL registers, named n, i, PV, PMT, and FV (page 9).

8. There are 20 NUMBERED storage registers, named with numbers 0 to 9 and .0 to .9 (page 8).

KEYING IN NUMBERS

Now that you know how to visualize the "insides" of your calculator, the next step is to put numbers into it.

First turn it on; the [ON] key is at the lower left (and it's also the "off" key).

Now, the rule for keying in a number is simple. Whenever you press the digit keys, the number you form will be put into the X–register (and into the display, right?).

You don't have to press any other keys.

Try This: Key in 1.234567890

Solution: Press [1] [.] [2] [3] [4] [5] [6] [7] [8] [9] [0]

That's all. You're done.

ADJUSTING THE NUMBER OF DECIMAL PLACES

Look again at the display.

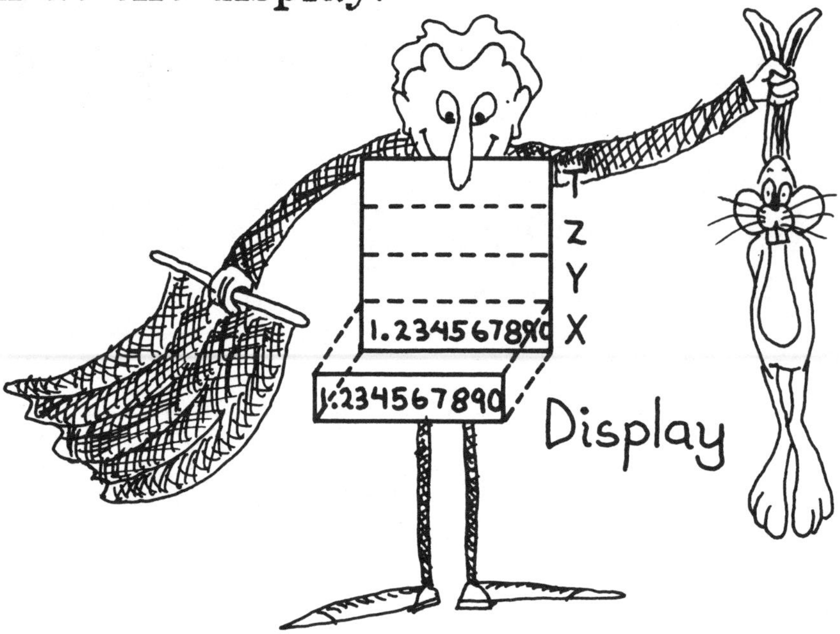

As you know, the display is like a window over the X–register. Whenever you're keying in a number, this window slides open so that you can see exactly what you're keying into the X–register.

But, usually, you don't want to see every decimal place of calculated results. You already know that the display can screen some of those digits. For example, if you were to ask the calculator to show you only 4 decimal places of the number in the X–register, it would show you: 1.2346

The last digit gets rounded to 6.

BUT REMEMBER! The display is doing this rounding. The number in the X–register is NOT rounded.

Try that: Set the display to show you only 4 decimal places of the number 1.234567890.

Solution: Press [f] 4

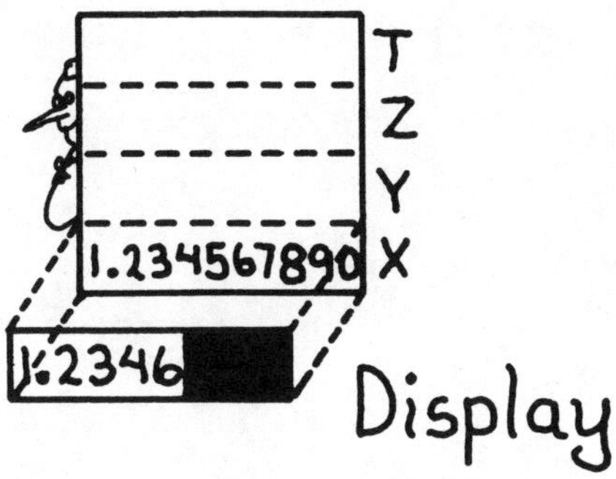

The window closes down so that the number in the display becomes 1.2346, but the number in the X–register remains 1.234567890.

And any calculation will use ALL 10 digits of this number.

That's the way it is with HP calculators. They use and store 10–digit numbers—ALWAYS.

It's important to remember that the calculator always stores and uses ten–digit numbers.

For example, suppose that the number in the X–register is 1.234567890, but the display is showing you only 4 decimal places (just as you requested): 1.2346

Suppose you wrote it down as an intermediate result and then used it later for another calculation. To do so, you key in 1.2346.

Wrong!

What you keyed in was 1.2346(00000), which is incorrect and will produce incorrect subsequent results. You won't even be able to work backwards to verify your original numbers!

Of course, by the time you're finished with this course, you won't feel the need to write down intermediate results anyway.

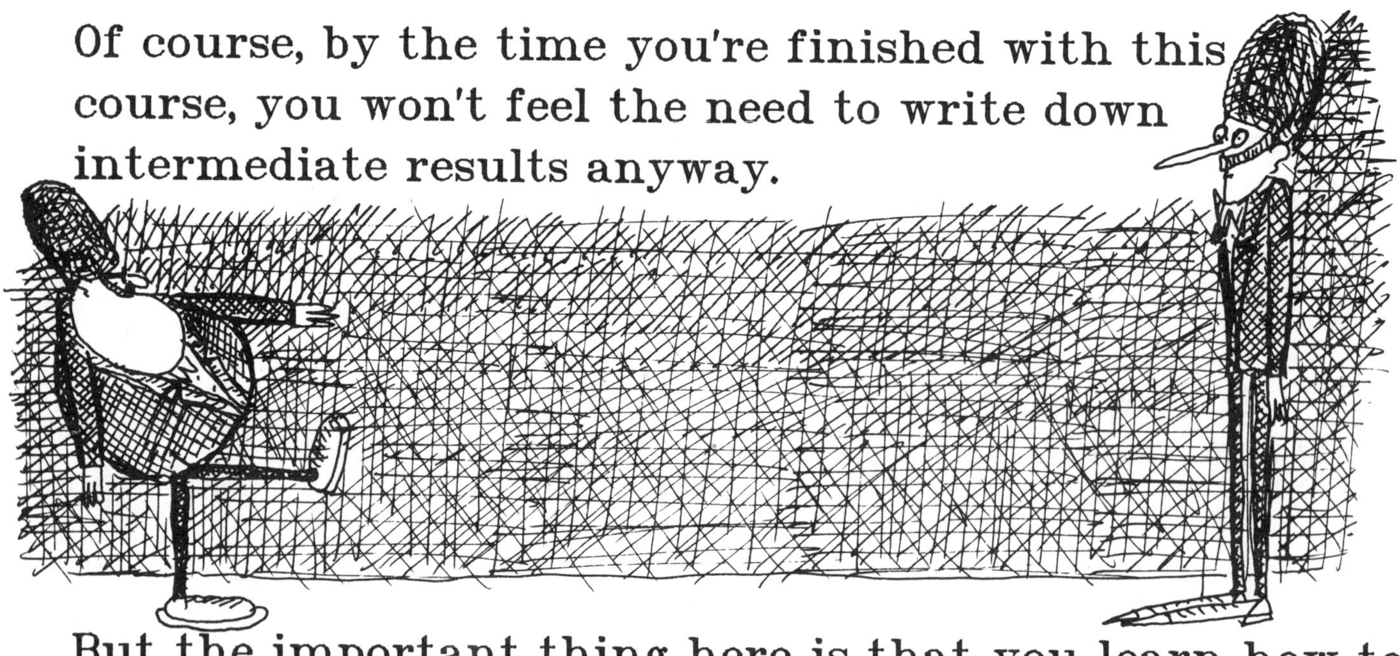

But the important thing here is that you learn how to change the display setting. So...

Try this: Adjust the display to show you 2 decimal places.

Solution: [f] 2

Try This: Set the display to show 9 decimal places.

Solution: [f] 9

Get the idea? Good. Now, set the display to whatever is comfortable for you.

And blitz on ahead...!

BEYOND THE X–REGISTER

Try This: Key in 100 to the X–register.

Solution: Press [1] [0] [0]. That's all.

Once you have a number in the X–register, there are three things you can do with it.

1. Store it in another register.

2. Use it to perform some calculation.

3. Erase it.

The first of these options is to store that number somewhere else. (If you already know about the STO and RCL keys, turn to page 25.)

STORING NUMBERS

Try this: Put that 100 into register 2.

Solution: [STO] 2

Notice what this [STO] key does: the number that's stored is ALWAYS the one that's in the X–register.

Also, the [STO] process is a copying process, not a transferring process. That 100 is now in register 2, but it's still in the X–register as well. (You still see 100 in the display.)

To store into a numbered register, all you do is press [STO] and then name the register: [STO] [1], [STO] [.] [9], etc.

The same is true for the FINANCIAL registers. If you want to store a copy of that 100 (which is still in the X–register) into the register named FV, just press [STO] [FV]. Try it.

The procedure is the same for the other financial registers: [STO] [n], [STO] [i], etc. (There is a storage shortcut when you're dealing with the financial registers, but that's discussed later.)

RECALLING NUMBERS

Yes, Virginia, there is a matching key: [RCL] (recall).

This key recalls a number--from any register you name--back to the X-register.

Key a 5 into the X-register. Now [RCL] [FV] brings to the X-register the 100 that you just stored in the FV-register.

And [RCL] makes copies of numbers--just like [STO] does. After you press [RCL] [FV], there's still a 100 in the FV-register.

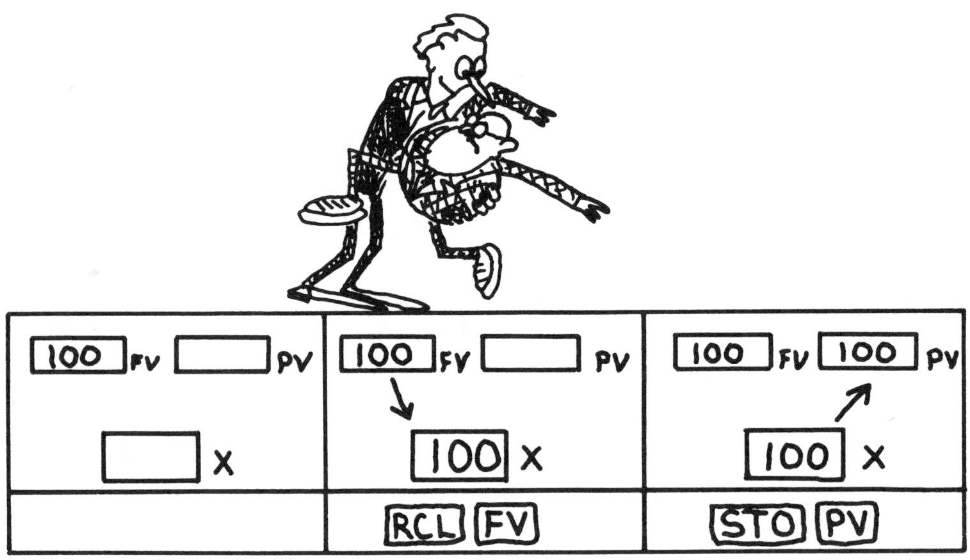

[STO] and [RCL] allow you to move numbers from one register to another. If you want to move the number from the FV-register to the PV-register, you key [RCL] [FV], [STO] [PV].

Here's that list again. Once you get a number into the X–register (either by recalling it or keying it in), you can:

1. Store it in another register.
2. Use it in some calculation.
3. Erase it.

Now you know all about the first entry in that list. The second entry is essentially the meat of this course. For an introduction, take a look at one of the simpler calculations you can perform on a number as it sits in the X–register.

Try This: Change that 100 to –100.

Solution: [CHS] (NOT the [–] key). [CHS] is the "CHange Sign" key, and it always operates on the number in the X–register.

Press [CHS] again. What happens?

This is just one example to show how most of the other calculation keys work. They somehow operate on the number in the X–register (and sometimes other registers, too).

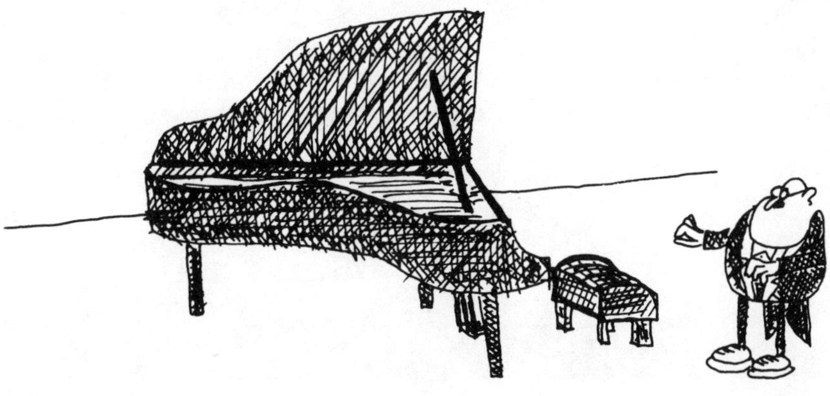

Keep this in mind and look again at the keyboard.

Notice that there are more operations shown on the keyboard than there are keys. But how does one "get at" all those operations?

Well, it's time to introduce the "prefix keys."

(If you already know about prefix keys, flip ahead to page 32.)

PREFIX KEYS

There are two prefix keys on the HP-12C. They are colored gold and blue and are marked [f] and [g], respectively.

Pressing a prefix key is much like shifting to UPPER CASE on a typewriter, except you DON'T have to hold down prefix keys, and you don't usually press prefix keys with your little finger.

Notice that all the "upper case" operations are printed in gold or blue (above the key or on it). These colors correspond to the color of the correct prefix keys you need to press first.

Just press and release the gold or blue prefix key. Then select your gold or blue operation.

(It's nice that HP printed f and g on the prefix keys, especially for people who publish books in black and white.)

Try This: What would you do if, for some reason, you wanted to clear all the FINancial registers?

Solution: Press [f] CLEAR [FIN]

You may be wondering where the CLEAR FIN key is. Well, notice the five keys--with gold printing above them--that look like this:

That gold bracket notation really signifies this:

Since these operations are printed in gold, you would press the gold [f] key first (and release it, of course).

Then press the key with the gold FIN printed above it, because you know this is the CLEAR [FIN] key.

You're done.

Clearing a register is the same thing as storing a zero in that register. When you clear X, the calculator puts a zero in the X–register. When you press [f] CLEAR [FIN], it put zeroes in all the FINancial registers.

A good thing to notice is that when you press [g], a little g comes on in the display, indicating that all the keys are taking their blue meanings. Then, if you press [f], the g is replaced by an f in the display (the keys have their gold meanings).

Play around with it for a while.

Notes

ANOTHER QUICK REVIEW

Again, be sure of the answers to these before you go on. (The answers are on the next page.)

1. Which two keys provide a "matched set" of operations that allow you to store or recall numbers?

2. Which stack register is always involved with storing and recalling?

3. Do these operations copy or transfer numbers?

4. How do you change the sign of a number (from positive to negative or vice versa)? In which register must this number be in order to do this?

5. What is a prefix key, and how does it work?

6. How many prefix keys are on your calculator? Which ones are they?

MORE QUICK ANSWERS

1. The two keys are [STO] and [RCL] (Pages 22–23).

2. These operations always use the X–register.

3. They copy numbers.

4. Use the [CHS] key. The number you want to change must be in the X–register (see page 25).

5. A prefix key is a key you must press (and release) before selecting the alternate ("UPPER CASE") operations on any key (pages 27–28).

6. There are 2 prefix keys: the gold [f] and the blue [g].

So, what do you know by now?

A. You know how to picture the insides of your calculator.

B. You know how to put numbers into it.

C. You know that once a number is in the X–register, you can:

1. STOre it.
2. Perform operations and calculations with it.
3. Clear it.

But you haven't seen many calculations yet, have you? What about the most common calculations of all?

WHAT ABOUT PLAIN OLD–FASHIONED ARITHMETIC?!?

(time for brass tacks)

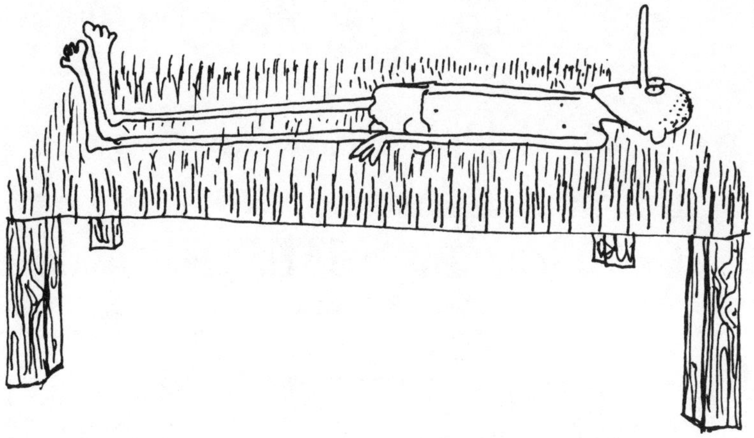

The Beauty Of The Stack
(a.k.a. PLAIN OLD–FASHIONED ARITHMETIC)

Whenever you do arithmetic on your HP financial calculator, you're using that special set of four linked storage registers called "the stack."

This stack is what makes HP calculators so much easier to use than the other leading brands. Solving complicated arithmetic problems will be easier than you ever imagined, and you'll wonder how anyone could want a calculator that doesn't have a "stack."

When you're using the stack to work out an answer to a complicated problem, you never have to write down intermediate answers, nor do you have to store them, because intermediate results are stored automatically (as you generate them) by the actions of the stack.

Another thing that makes the stack so easy is that you never have to use parentheses. Notice that there are no parentheses keys on the keyboard.

(Of course, if you're already thoroughly up to speed on the stack, skip ahead to page 60.)

And relax; by the end of this section, you'll know how it all works, and you won't even need to be thinking about what's happening. The stack will become automatic for you--it's THAT good.

But as with any clever tool, you have to learn how to use it first.

So how does the stack work?

Well, you've already seen a picture like this:

This is a good way to "picture" the stack in your mind: four registers stacked up.

And as you know, the number you see in the display is always the number in the X–register (usually a rounded version of that number).

You can't see the Y–, Z–, and T–registers, but they're as real and as important as the X–register.

So remember that diagram (above).

(Actually, after this section, you'll never forget it.)

Here's a typical arithmetic problem:

$$\begin{array}{r} 24.00 \\ \underline{\times\, 3.25} \end{array}$$

Notice how the numbers are stacked up, and how the operation can be the last thing you write down.

Well, guess what....

Here's how you solve that problem on an HP calculator:

24 [ENTER] 3.25 [X]

The operation comes LAST.

Watch what happens in the stack.

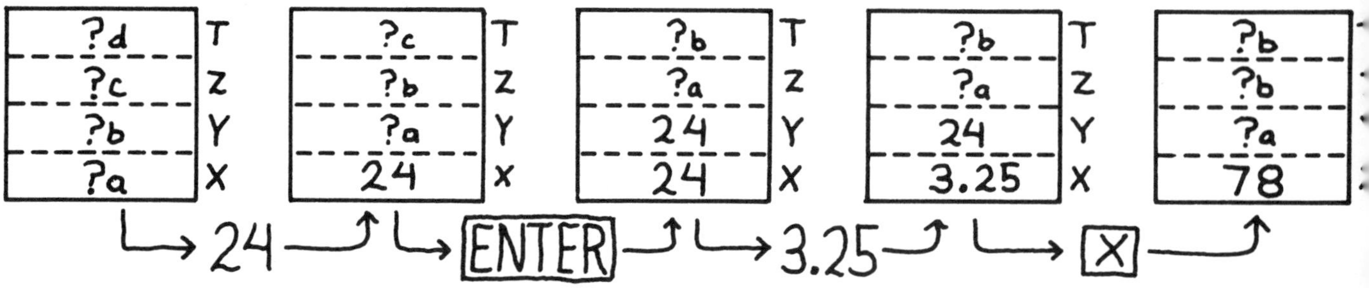

(?a, ?b, etc. mean "some number is there but it doesn't matter what it is.")

Study this for a while. Look at each stack diagram and at the changes that occur between steps.

Try This: Divide that 78 by 3:

Solution: 3 ÷

The 78 is already in the stack, so you don't need to key it in. You just need to put the 3 "underneath" it and then divide.

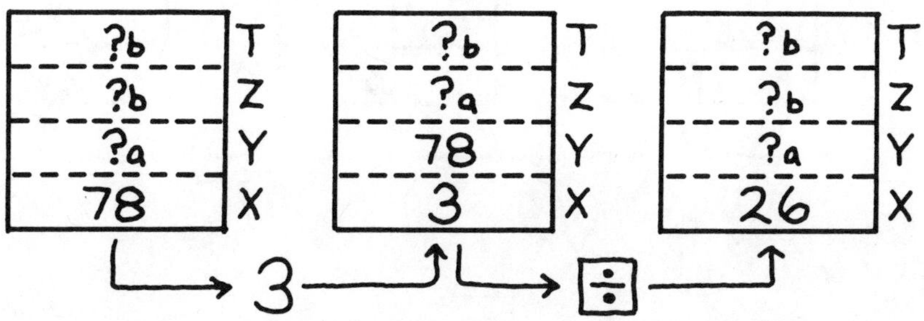

So you've already worked out a problem that looks like this:

$$\frac{(24 \times 3.25)}{3}$$

(No need for parentheses keys!)

Here's how the stack looks as you solve the whole thing:

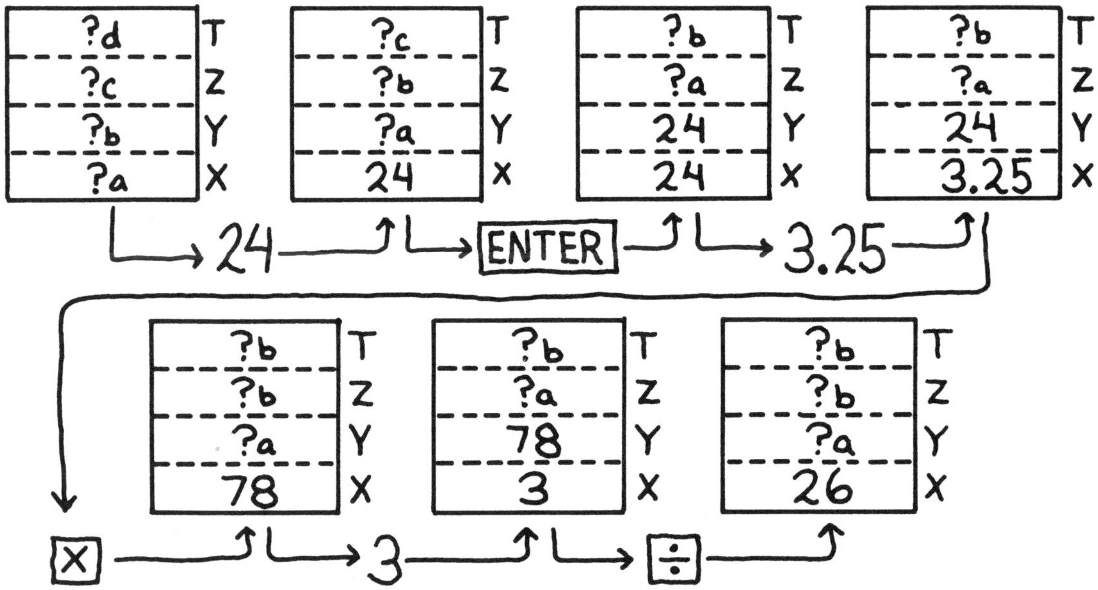

Question: Why don't you need to press ENTER after the ⊠?

(If you know the answer to this, and you're SURE you want to skip a fine discussion of stack–lift and ENTER, then go ahead to page 48.)

But if you're not sure about all this, STEP THIS WAY....

Look at the first two steps of that solution:

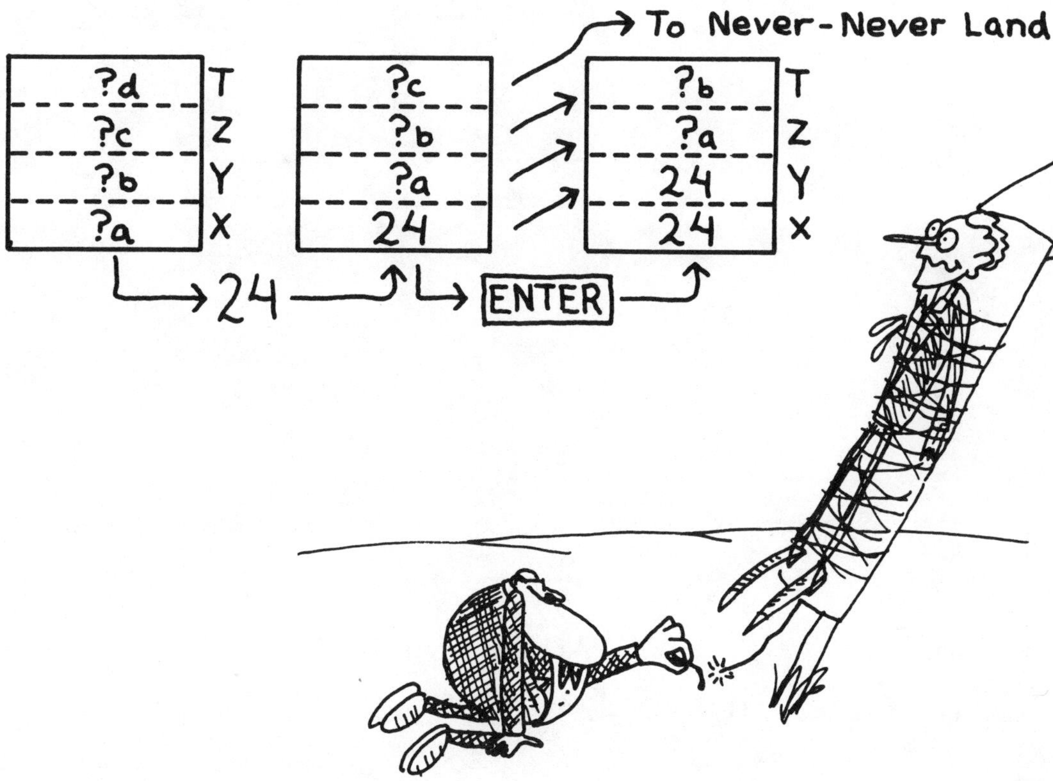

Notice what ENTER does to the stack.

ENTER CAUSES A STACK–LIFT.

That is, the numbers in the X–, Y–, and Z–registers each get bumped up one notch, and the number in the T–register is gone for good.

This process is called a STACK–LIFT.

Now look at the next step where you key in 3.25:

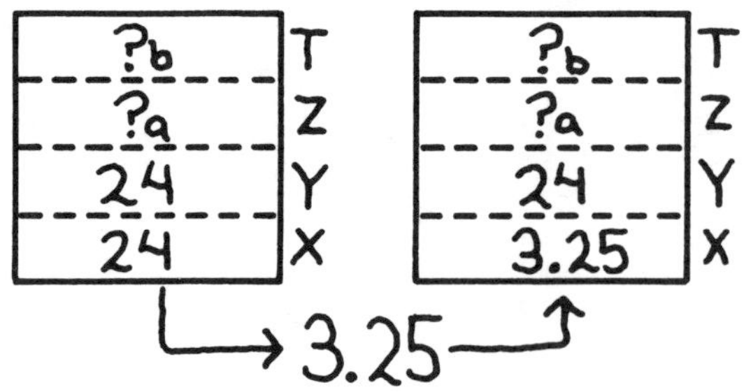

Question: Does keying in a number right after [ENTER] cause a stack–lift?

Answer: NO!

The 3.25 simply replaces the 24 in the X–register.

That's the other thing [ENTER] does:

[ENTER] leaves the stack DISABLED. That is, if you key in a number immediately after pressing [ENTER], that number will not cause a stack–lift. The stack won't lift because [ENTER] made it "unable" to do so.

Therefore, the number you key in will replace what's in the X–register, rather than lifting it to the Y–register.

Now, look at the next two steps in the solution:

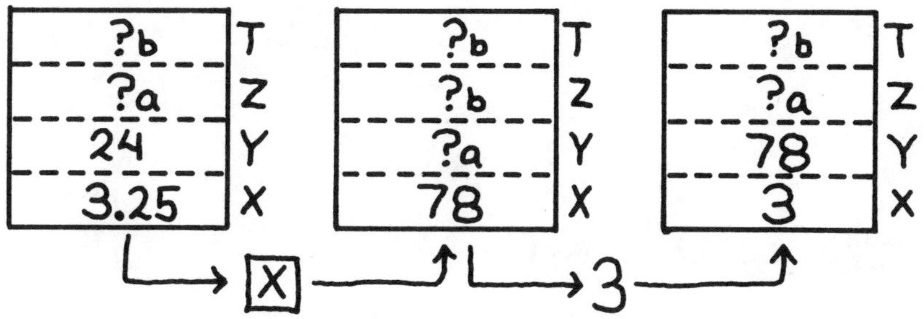

Question: Does keying in a number after the X cause a stack–lift?

Answer: YES!!!

The X (multiply) operation––like most others––always leaves the stack ENABLED. This means that if you key in a number, the number previously in the X–register is lifted to the Y–register.

If the stack is ENabled, when you key in a number, the stack lifts.

If the stack has been DISabled by ENTER, then when you key in a number, the stack doesn't lift.

It's as simple as that. This is how intermediate results are saved automatically.

(If you're confused, take a break. Have a cup of tea. When you come back, start here.)

Look at ENTER a little bit more:

Try to set the stack up like this:

Solution: 8 ENTER 6.9 ENTER 12.4 ENTER 3.9

Here's what the stack does:

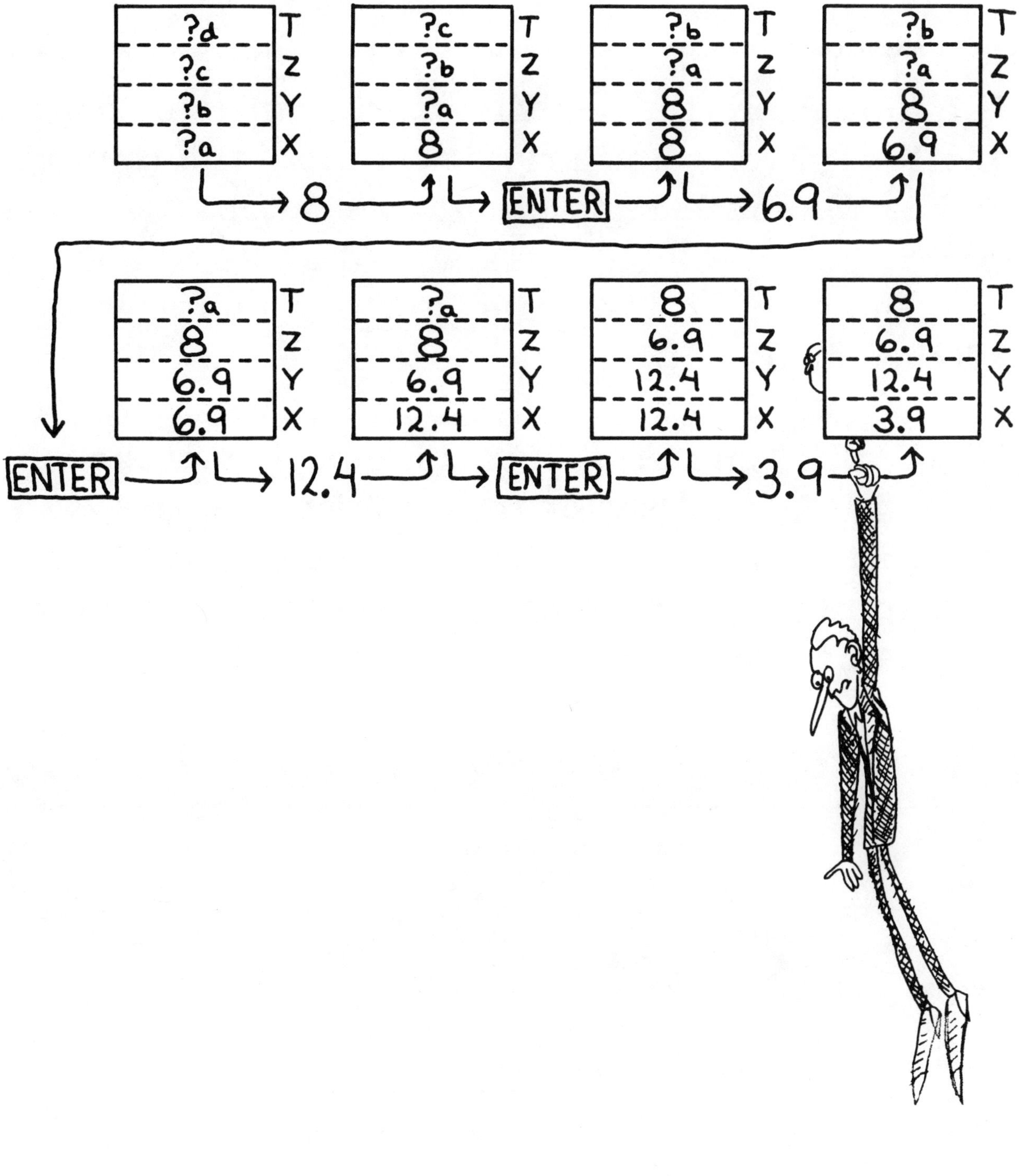

As you can see, ENTER does two things (in this order):

1. IT ALWAYS CAUSES A STACK–LIFT: it makes a copy of the number in the X–register and puts this copy into the Y–register. Similarly, it "bumps" the numbers in the Y–, and Z–registers up one notch.

   And the value in the T–register is gone for good after a stack–lift.

2. IT DISABLES THE STACK: if the next keystroke is keying in a number (or recalling one) to the X–register, the stack will be "unable" to lift. So the number previously in the X–register is replaced by the new number (not "bumped up").

ENTER...

1. CAUSES a stack–lift

2. DISABLES the stack.

Simple, right?

Before you go on, be sure that your stack now looks like this (use the procedure on page 45):

Suppose you want to divide that 3.9 (in the X–register) by 2 . The correct keystrokes would be...

2 [÷], right?

Wrong. You've keyed in 3.9 but you've done nothing else––nothing to tell your calculator that you're finished with that number and that you want to key in a 2.

That's what [ENTER] is for: it saves the first number by putting a copy in the Y–register. And it "disables" the stack so that the second number will "write over" what's in the X–register without affecting Y, Z, and T.

But suppose you forgot all that and (heaven forbid!) made a mistake. Suppose you did this:

8 ENTER 6.9 ENTER 12.4 ENTER 3.9

You suddenly decide to divide that 3.9 by 2...so you press 2.

Here's what the stack does:

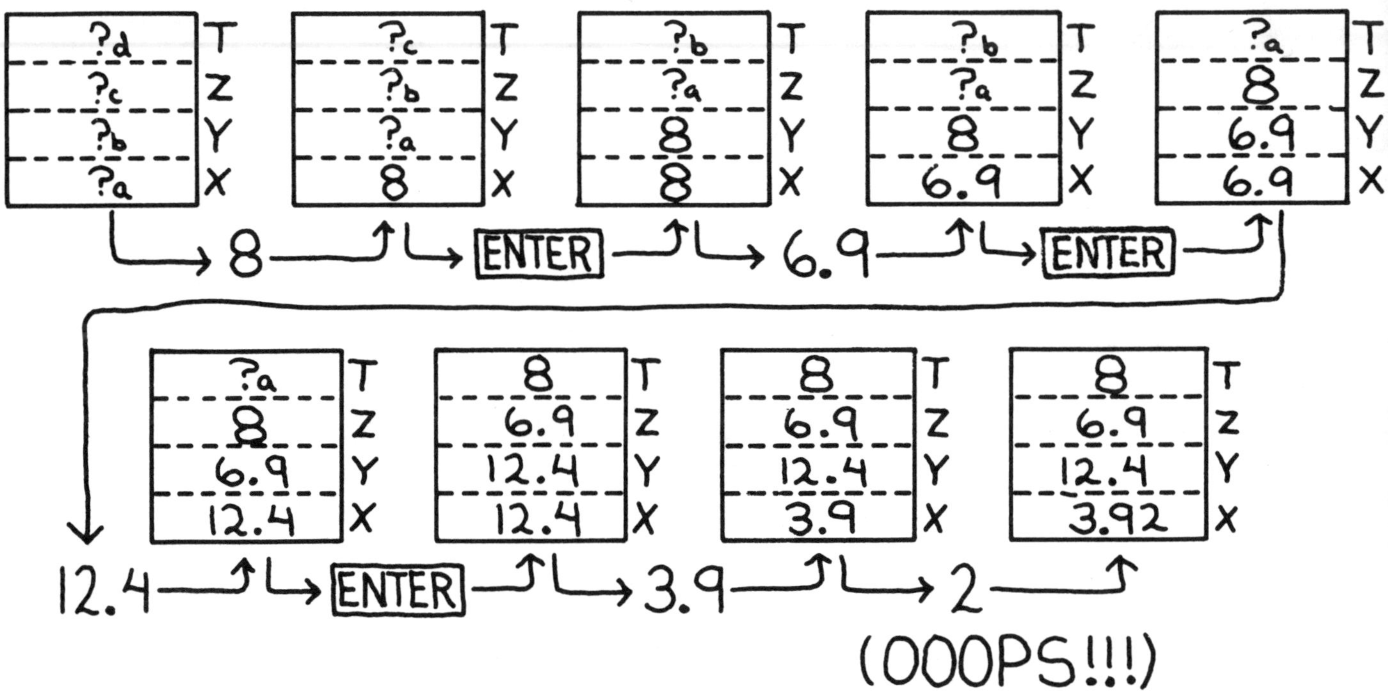

NOW you've done it....

Try to correct your mistake. Put the stack back to its previous form:

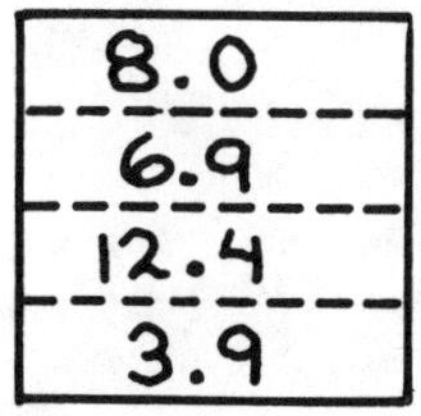

Solution: [CLX] 3.9

What's this [CLX] key?

Simple: [CLX] just puts a zero in the X–register.

AND IT DISABLES THE STACK so you can key in the correct number.

Watch the stack:

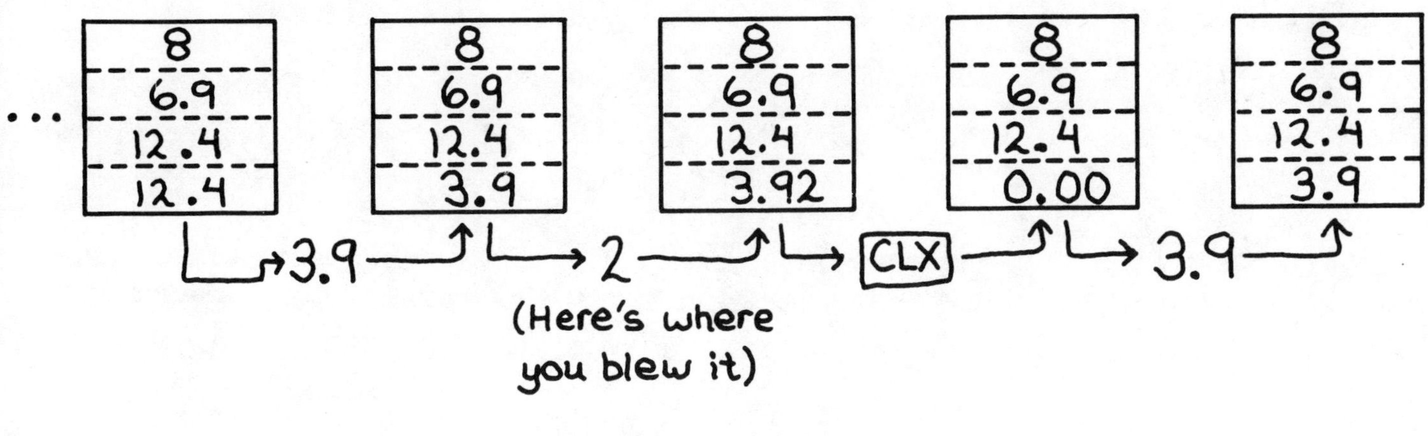

Question: Does a stack–lift occur when you key in that last 3.9?

Answer: NO!
That must mean that [CLX] disables the stack (it does).

Now finish the problem: Divide that 3.9 by 2.

Solution: [ENTER] 2 [÷]

No sweat, right?

Chisel this in stone:

[ENTER] and [CLX] are the only two common stack operations that DISABLE the stack.

Just about any other operation on your HP calculator will leave the stack ENABLED.

What are some of these operations?

Try This: What if you want to see the rest of the numbers in the stack?

Solution: Use the [R↓] "roll–down" key.

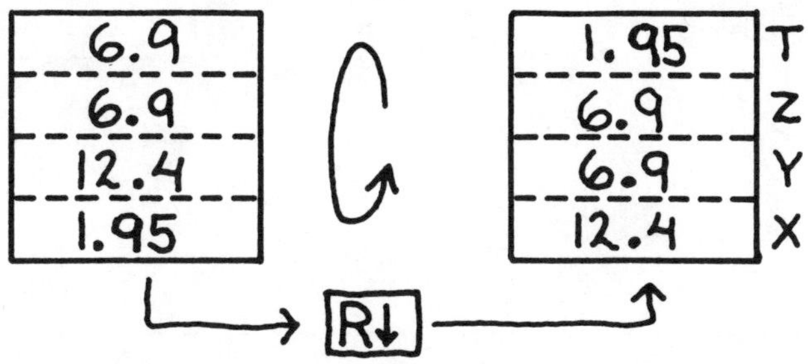

See why it's called "roll–down?"

All the numbers are preserved, but a new one is rolled down into the X–register.

Question: The stack is left ENABLED by the [R↓] operation What happens when you key in the number 3.9?

Solution: The stack lifts.

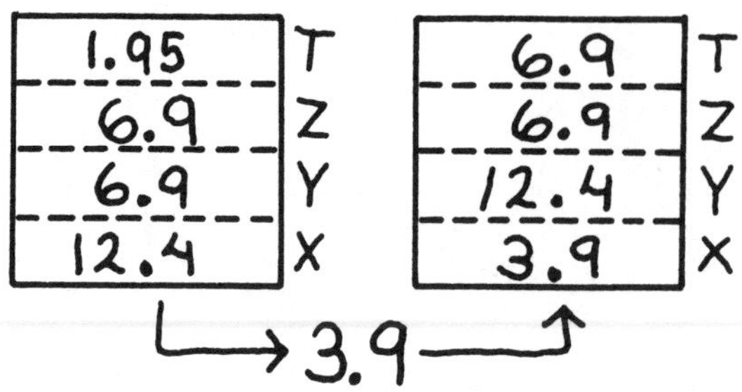

Question: What do you suppose the [X<>Y] ("X–exchange–Y") key does?

Answer: You guessed it! Watch:

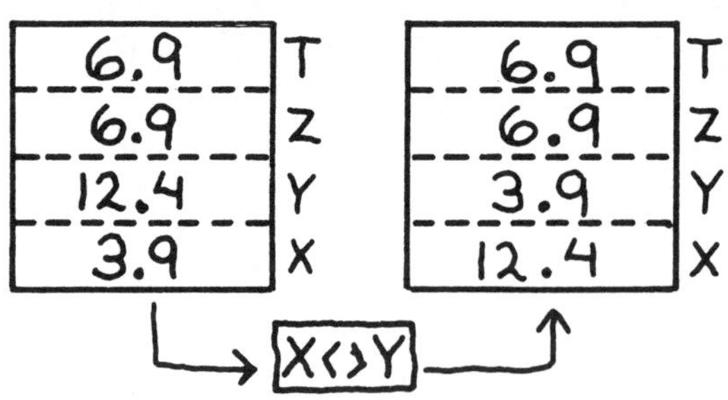

Again, the stack is left enabled.

THE ARITHMETIC OPERATIONS

Question: If the stack looks like this:

6.9	T
6.9	Z
3.9	Y
12.4	X

What happens when you press [+]?

Answer:

6.9	T
6.9	Z
3.9	Y
12.4	X

→ [+] →

6.9	T
6.9	Z
6.9	Y
16.3	X

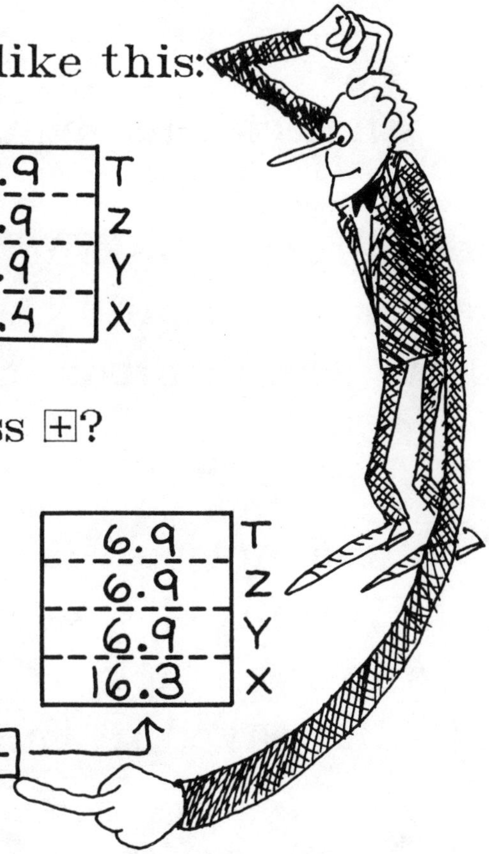

The arithmetic operations use the numbers in the X– and Y–registers, and the result ends up in the X–register, ALWAYS!

And look what else happens:

The stack "drops," making a copy of the T–register into the Z–register, and the Z–register into the Y–register. The number in the T–register stays the same.

And, of course, notice that the stack is left ENABLED. You press [+], get a result, then key in a number, and the stack will lift. Your result is automatically saved in the Y–register.

Add these words and phrases to your HP vocabulary:

1. Stack–lift.

2. Stack is enabled.

3. Stack is disabled.

Now try to solve this problem: $\frac{(7 \times 6.3) - 9}{7.5 + 12} + 4$

Solution: 7 ENTER 6.3 × 9 − 7.5 ENTER 12 +
÷ 4 +   Answer: 5.80

Piece of cake, right?

Here's what happens in the stack. Study it carefully and practice your new vocabulary. Where is the stack enabled? Where is a stack–lift occurring?

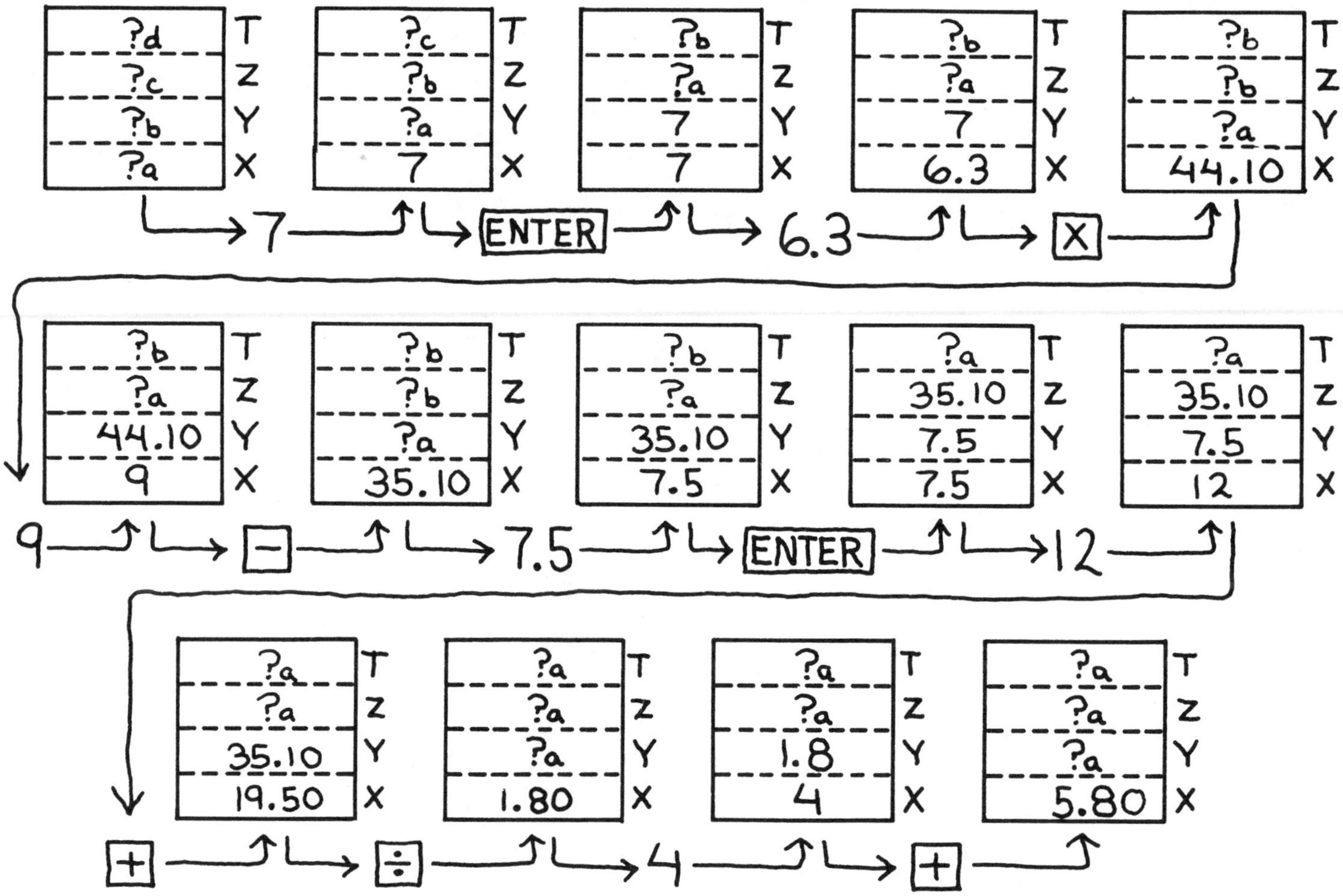

("Wow...this is great!")

And here are a couple more good operations to know:

Try This: Find the "square root" of 16.

Solution: 16 [g] [$\sqrt{x}$]

You keyed 16 into the X–register and pressed [g] [$\sqrt{x}$]. Now $\sqrt{16}$ is in the X–register. Plain and simple.

Try this: Find 4^3 (four raised to the third power).

Solution: 3 [y^x]

Since 4 was already in the X–register, you key in 3, which bumps the 4 up to the Y–register. Then [y^x] (say "y–to–the–x") raises the number in the Y–register to the power in the X–register.

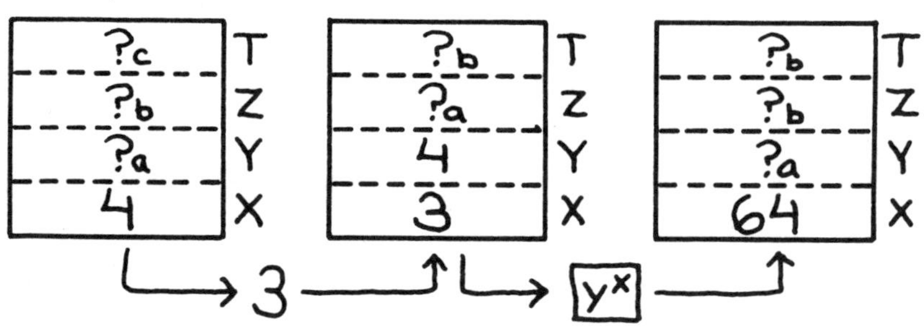

STACK QUIZ

1. Name two keys that DISABLE the stack. And what happens when you key in a number right after pressing one of these keys?

2. Does the following sequence fill the stack with zeroes? [CLX] 0 [CLX] 0 [CLX] 0 [CLX] 0

3. Look back on page 57. Would it make any difference if [ENTER] was pressed right after the [X]? How about after the first [+]?

4. What would the stack look like during the following keystrokes? (Assume that it was filled with zeroes to start with.)

   5 [ENTER] [ENTER] [+] 13 [X] 1 [CLX] [R↓] [CLX] 25
   [g] [√x] [÷]. What's the result?

(The answers are on the next pages, but don't look unless you have to.)

STACK ANSWERS

1. [ENTER] and [CLX] are the two keys you commonly use that will disable the stack. When you key in a number right after using [ENTER] or [CLX], that number will REPLACE the contents of the X–register rather than bumping it up to the Y–register.

2. No, this will not clear the stack. [CLX] disables the stack and prevents the zeroes from being pushed up into the stack. 0 [ENTER] [ENTER] [ENTER] is one way to clear the stack. But there's rarely a need to clear it at all, right?

3. No, it makes no difference after the [×] because the next key entry ([9]) would accomplish the same thing as [ENTER] [9].

   But pressing [ENTER] right after the first [+] will make a big difference. Think about it, and draw the stack diagrams if you aren't convinced.

4. Here's what the stack would look like:

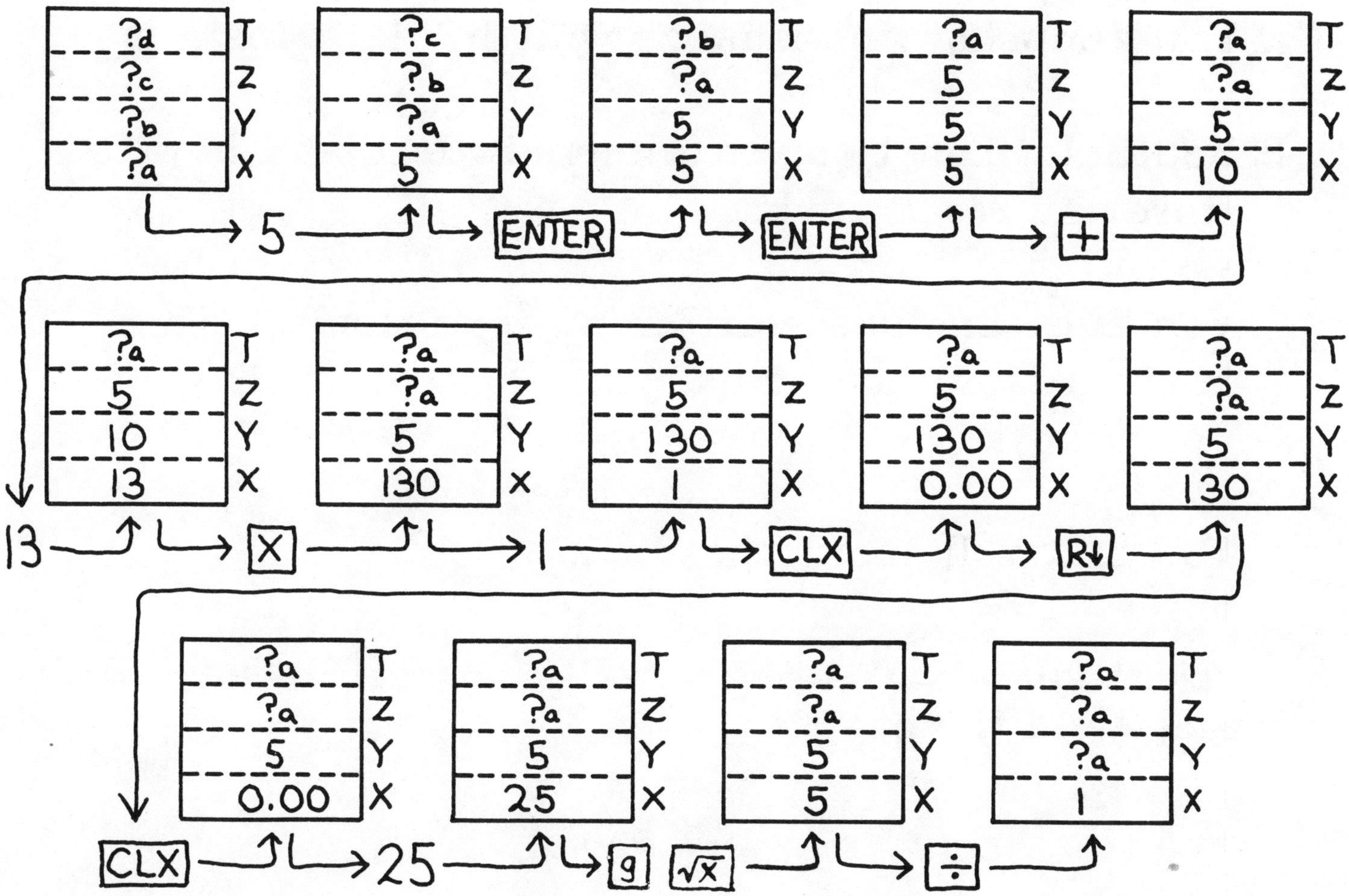

The result is 1.

So, take a look at where you've been so far:

A. You know how to visualize your HP–12C's insides.

B. You know how to put numbers into it, and how to store and recall them.

C. You know about the different operations on the keyboard and how to use them––with the help of prefix keys.

D. You know all about the stack.

And not only do you know about these things, but you understand them, yes?

Not bad.

But this is a financial calculator. It's time to look at those financial keys and how they work.

THE FINANCIAL KEYS AND HOW THEY WORK

Before learning to calculate the five financial numbers, you'd better learn how to store numbers in those 5 registers.

Remember how to put 100 into the [FV] register?

You already know that 100 [STO] [FV] works.

But so does this: 100 [FV]

(If you know all about this, skip to page 70.)

It's very important to know the details of this shortcut.

After you've keyed in a number, or recalled one, or performed almost any operation in the stack, you can store the number in the X–register into any of the 5 financial registers by pressing the appropriate financial key. You DON'T need to press [STO].

Instead of	You can press
100 [STO] [FV]	100 [FV]
[RCL] 1 [STO] [n]	[RCL] 1 [n]
[X<>Y] [STO] [i]	[X<>Y] [i]
[+] [STO] [PMT]	[+] [PMT]

There's one other thing that's nice to know about using this shortcut. Back in the stack section you learned the phrases "stack is enabled" and "stack is disabled," and that ENTER and CLX are two common operations that disable the stack.

Well, surprise! When you use this shortcut to store a number in a financial register, THE STACK IS LEFT DISABLED. This comes in really handy when you're chaining together several financial calculations (but don't lose any sleep over it).

For now, concentrate on this: Just about the only time that you CANNOT use this shortcut to store into the financial registers is WHEN YOU HAVE JUST DONE SO.

100 [STO] [FV] [STO] [PV]	(This will store 100 into both the FV and PV registers.)
	BUT
100 [FV] [PV]	will not.

What it will do is calculate the correct number for PV, based upon the numbers currently in the n–, i–, PMT–, and FV–registers.

TO CALCULATE A FINANCIAL QUANTITY, YOU JUST PRESS THE APPROPRIATE FINANCIAL KEY.

You have to know about the STORAGE shortcut because it's the same keystroke you use for CALCULATION.

The only way the calculator knows whether you want to store or calculate a financial quantity is by what you did just prior to pressing the financial key:

If you just stored a financial value, then pressing any financial key will tell the machine to calculate.

BUT

If you just did something in the stack, then pressing a financial key will store the number in the X–register into that FINANCIAL register.

Tongue–tied? It doesn't matter if you can't say it––as long as you can do it.

Practice with this short quiz....

Notes

QUICK REVIEW

What effects will the following keystrokes have? Don't worry about the numerical answers. When will a number be stored, and when will one be calculated, recalled, etc.?

1. 100 [PV]
   [CHS] [FV]
   1 [n]
   [STO] [i]
   [PMT]

2. [RCL] [FV]
   [PV]
   [FV]

(See the next pages for answers.)

QUICK ANSWERS

Here are the results of those keystrokes. These are important to understand completely.

1. KEYSTROKES	EFFECT
100 [PV]	Keys in 100 to the X–register, then copies it into the PV–register.
[CHS] [FV]	Changes the 100 in the X–register to –100, then copies that into the FV–register.
1 [n]	1 is keyed into the X–register then copied to the n–register.
[STO] [i]	Copies the 1 in the X–register to the i–register.
[PMT]	Calculates the correct number for PMT based upon the other 4 numbers (n, i, PV, FV). This is a calculation instead of a storage, because you just stored a financial number (i).

2. KEYSTROKES	EFFECT
[RCL] [FV]	Recalls to the X–register (and the DISPLAY) a copy of the number contained in the FV–register.
[PV]	Stores (copies) that number from the X–register into the PV–register.
[FV]	Calculates the correct FV based upon the current values of n, i, PV, and PMT. Again, this is a calculation because a value was just stored in a FINANCIAL register.

The results of all financial calculations end up in the X–register as well as the correct financial register. For example, when you press [FV] the second time in the above example, the answer ends up in both the FV–register and the X–register.

There you have it. The operating fundamentals of an HP–12C in 72 easy pages (take a bow).

Now you know the essentials of what will happen when you press the keys of your calculator. You can picture where the numbers go, etc.

But...which keys should you press––and at which times––to solve your financial questions?!?

OK...it's time to consider some basic financial concepts and the ways to reduce those concepts to practice.

THE WONDERFUL WORLD OF FINANCE

WHAT ARE YOUR INTERESTS?

The whole world of finance is based upon one simple fact:

Borrowed money earns interest over time

So it's best to begin all this financial problem–solving with a quick reminder on how interest accrues.

(Don't leap over any of this just because it seems tedious. You'll find some subtleties you've not contemplated before, so grin and bear it.)

SIMPLE OR COMPOUND?

Basically, there are two forms of interest.

Simple interest.
Compound interest

Take a look:

A. Simple Interest

This is the less common method nowadays. With simple interest, the amount of money charged per period--as interest--is defined as a set percentage of the AMOUNT ORIGINALLY LOANED.

So, if $100.00 is loaned for 6 months at 1% per month, then the amount owed for interest will be exactly $6.00. For each month of the loan, the borrower must pay 1% of the original $100.00; that's $1.00 per month, for 6 months.

B. Compound Interest

This form is the much more widely used. With compound interest, the amount of money charged per period--as interest--is defined as a set percentage of the AMOUNT OWED AT THE BEGINNING OF THAT PERIOD.

Notice how compound interest differs from simple interest: Simple interest is a percentage of the amount originally loaned (originally owed), but compound interest is a percentage of the amount owed at some other point in time--and this point changes.

So, in the simple interest case, the borrower saw the $100.00 amount change to $101.00 after 1 month, 102.00 after 2 months, etc.

If, on the other hand, that $100.00 loan were 1% per month COMPOUND interest, the amount owed after 1 month would still be $101.00, but after 2 months, it would be $102.01; after 3 months, it would be 103.03; etc. The second month's interest is computed as 1% of the amount owed at the beginning of the second month--that is, 1% of $101.00, not 1% of $100.00.

Thus, interest is earned on interest earned previously, and thus the name--COMPOUND interest.

Since compound interest is the method of concern in most financial problems, it will be the main focus of the rest of this course.

WHENEVER YOU SEE THE WORD "INTEREST," YOU CAN ASSUME THAT IT'S COMPOUND INTEREST.

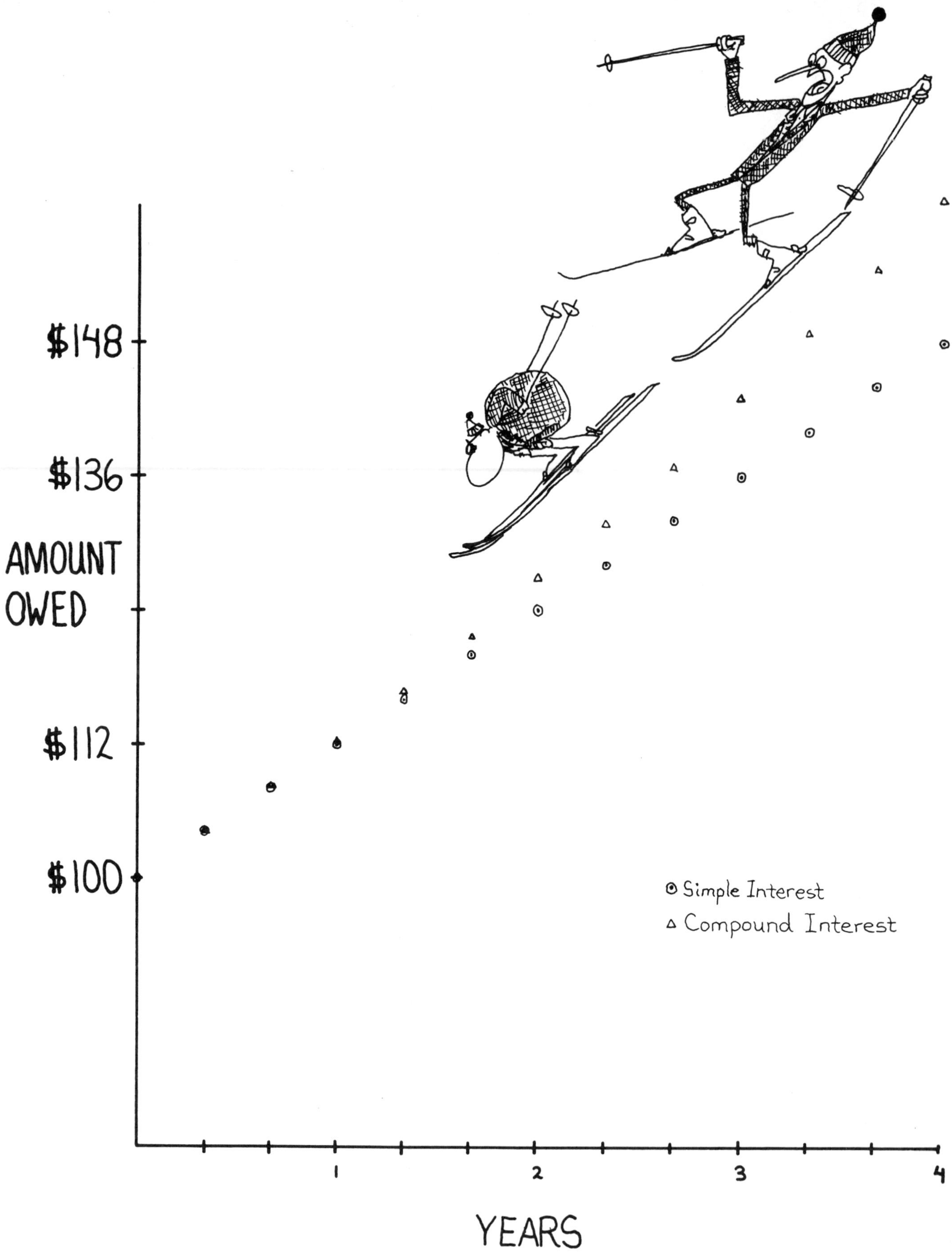

$148
$136
AMOUNT
OWED
$112
$100
YEARS
1
2
3
4
Simple Interest
Compound Interest

Now, all this may seem pretty obvious. But here are those subtleties that are too often overlooked:

SUBTLETY #1. In either form of interest, there is exactly one time period which is the Defined Interest Period (D.I.P.), and exactly one Defined Interest Rate (D.I.R.) for that period.

The example with the $100.00 specifically states that interest accrues "at 1% per month." So the D.I.P. is 1 month, and the D.I.R. is 1% (one percent).

However, it's conventional to quote interest rates on an annual basis. A bank would take that 1%, multiply it by 12 (months in a year), and say "12% Annual Percentage Rate (A.P.R.)." But this A.P.R. is just symbolic. THE BANK WOULD NEVER USE THE A.P.R. IN ITS CALCULATIONS. IT WOULD ALWAYS DIVIDE IT BY 12 FIRST AND THEN USE THIS D.I.R. THE A.P.R. IS A CONVENIENT APPROXIMATION.

Always make sure you know the D.I.R. and D.I.P. before you start a financial calculation.

SUBTLETY #2. In that $100.00 example, no mention was made of the amount owed after 2.5 months, or 3.75 months or 4.19 months, etc.

The D.I.R. and D.I.P. define only what the loan balance will be at one point in each period. There must be other definitions to determine how that balance changes between those points.

That's why the points on the graph on page 79 aren't connected with lines. Nobody can tell from the D.I.R. and D.I.P. how those lines should be drawn.

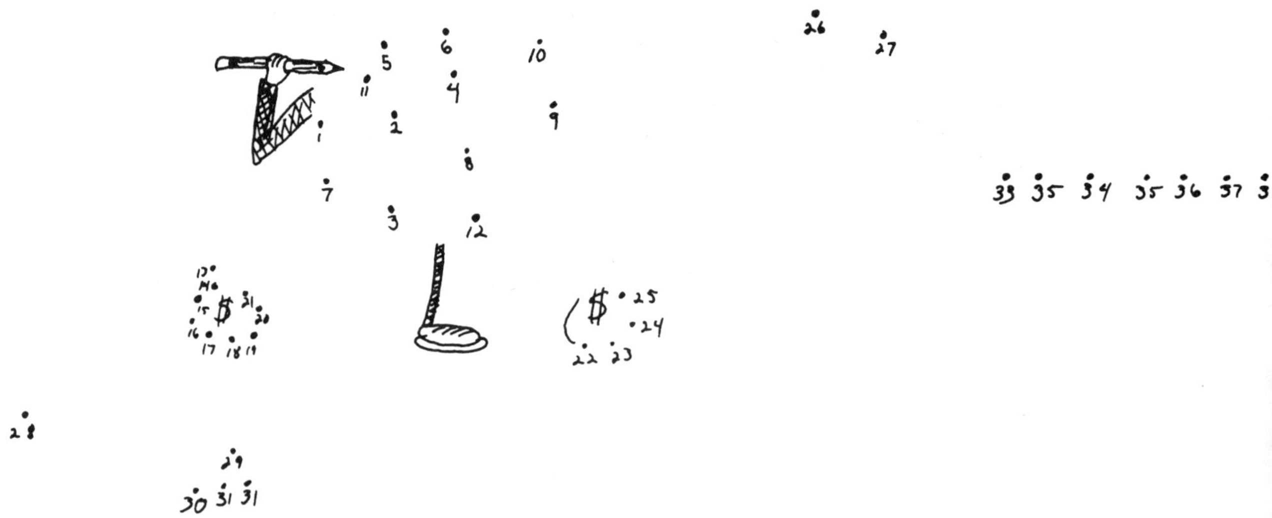

With these subtleties in mind, you can now proceed in solving problems with your Financial Calculator.

The problem–solving method goes like this:

1. Define the problem! Understand clearly what's known and what's unknown.

2. Present the right question to your Financial Calculator––in terms it can understand––so that it can find that unknown for you.

Look at these two steps in detail....

1. Define the problem!

You may not believe this, but this is the most important and most difficult part of all. Too many financial mistakes have been made because people have not clearly described the question--to themselves! They get too impatient to start punching buttons.

A calculator minimizes the amount of paper you have to use. BUT, it is not a substitute for paper!

Concentrate on defining a problem first. As you know, a picture is worth at least a thousand words (more if you allow for inflation), especially when you're trying to reduce a financial contract or proposal to its bare essentials.

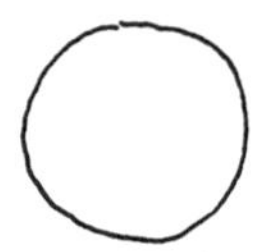

That's why a cash-flow diagram is so useful. It tells you at a glance what the facts are--without all the jargon and confusion of a verbal description.

So...what's a cash-flow diagram?

This is a cash–flow diagram:

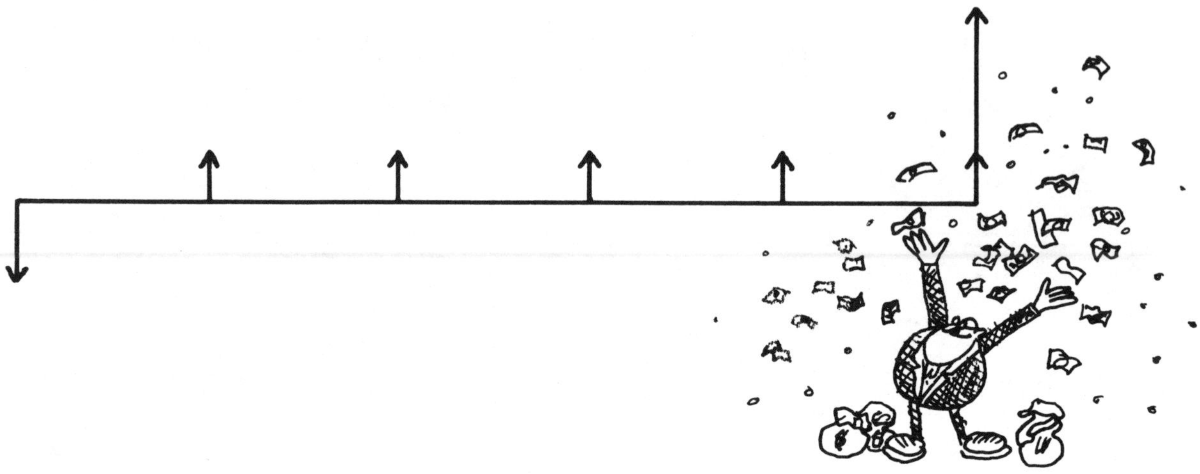

You'll see a lot of these from now on. Cash–flow diagrams are the easiest way to define and understand a financial problem.

The first thing to do in performing any financial calculation is...

draw a cash–flow diagram!

Write this in stone. It should become a reflex.

"OK, but how do I draw these diagrams, anyway? I'm not an artist, you know!"

That's all right—these diagrams are merely rough pictures to help you visualize the problem. But to make them really useful you should know the rules.

There are five rules for drawing a cash-flow diagram:

1. Always pick the perspective of either a borrower or a lender on one cash-flow diagram. (One could say "either a borrower or a lender be," but one would not want to be embarrassed, so one would keep it to oneself.)

   If you're buying money market shares, or putting money in a savings account, you should consider yourself a lender. If you're taking out a loan to buy a house, you're a borrower.

   The same loan will look different on a cash-flow diagram depending upon whether you're the lender or the borrower. So in drawing the picture, pick one perspective and keep it. And for money's sake, don't change your mind halfway through!

2. Once you've picked your perspective, the directions of the vertical arrows then denote the directions of the transactions. An upward arrow means that you receive money; a downward arrow means that you pay money.

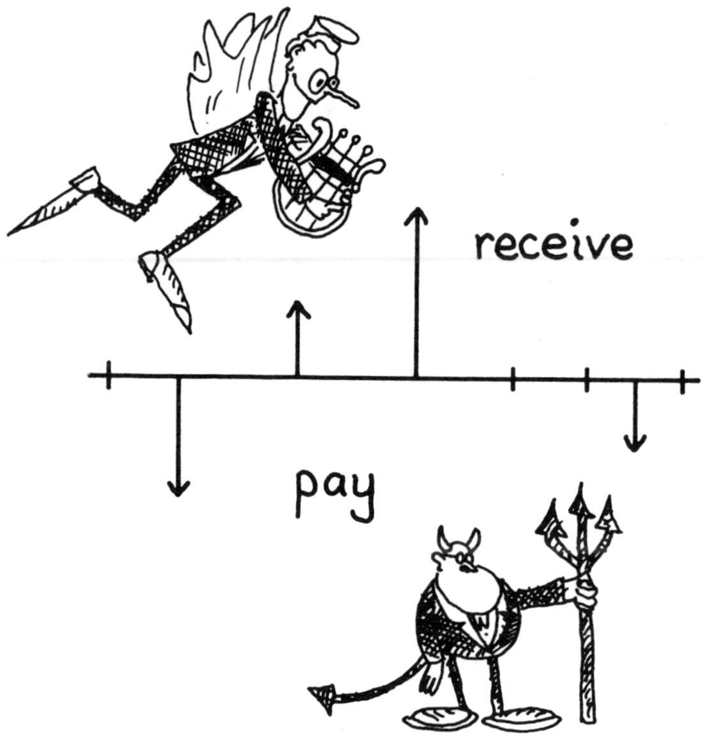

3. The lengths of these vertical arrows should reflect the amounts of the transactions. A longer arrow means more money (but don't quibble over pennies and millimeters if the general idea is clear).

4. The horizontal direction represents time (flowing from left to right). Usually, this line is marked at regular intervals to denote the D.I.P.'s. This makes sense because the calculators are equipped to handle only regularly occurring cash–flows.

5. Whenever you have multiple transactions that occur simultaneously, you can add them all together to obtain one net transaction. Thus:

is the same as:

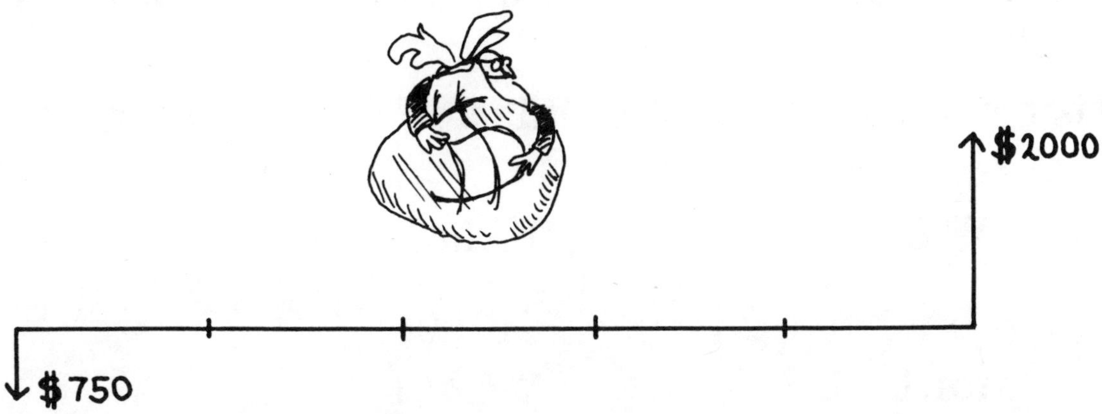

Those are the rules for drawing cash–flow diagrams. You'll get plenty of practice drawing these diagrams in the upcoming examples, so don't worry about being able to recite these rules on cue.

Now, here's the real beauty of the cash–flow diagram: You can ADJUST it to make it simpler. With a cash–flow diagram, you can get a clear picture of the advantages or disadvantages of different options offered in a financial situation.

How does this work?

Well, remember that $100.00 loan for 6 months?

After each month, the balance owed is slightly more:

AFTER	BALANCE IS
month 1	$101.00
month 2	$102.01
month 3	$103.03
month 4	$104.06
month 5	$105.10
month 6	$106.15

Suppose you could decide to repay the loan at any given month. You could draw six different versions of the loan:

Think of this as playing "what–if?" with the repayment. "What if I paid now? What if I waited three more months?", etc.

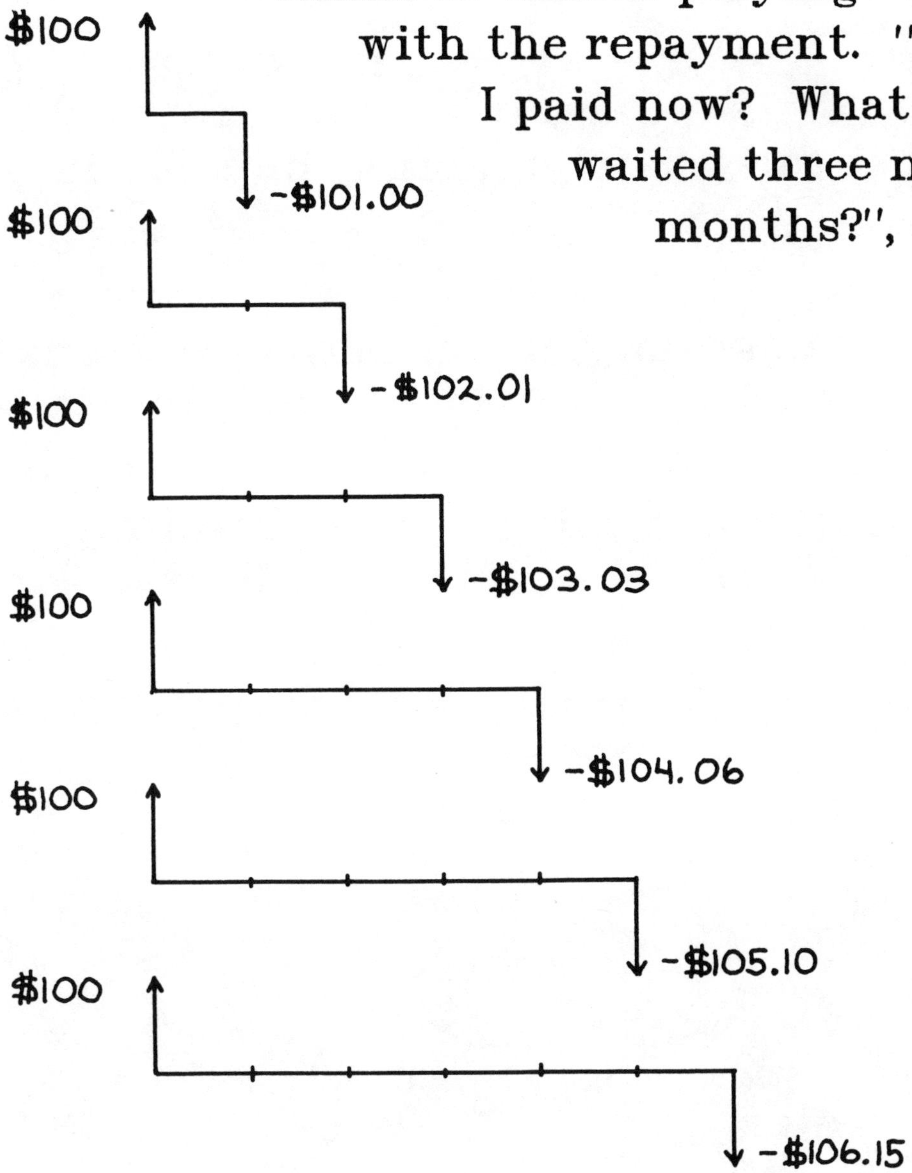

And, as you ponder, you're sliding that repayment up and down the timeline. And, wherever you put it, the picture is accurate, as long as you adjust the amount to account for the interest accrued.

The only thing that determines how that transaction shrinks or grows (as you slide it around) is the prevailing interest rate.

It's pretty easy to see how this "sliding" affects this simple case. But it works for more complicated cash–flow situations, too.

THAT'S where it's really handy. Here's the trick in a nutshell:

On any cash–flow diagram you can move any transaction forward or backward in time and maintain COMPLETE accuracy––provided that you let that transaction grow or shrink according to the prevailing interest rate.

That's about all there is to know about cash–flow diagrams. You'll always draw a diagram before keying a problem into your calculator, because the cash–flow diagram is the first step to translating your problem to the calculator's "language." After a while, of course, for the simpler problems, you may draw this picture just in your mind, not with pencil and paper.

But for the more complicated situations, it's best to take some time to put a cash–flow diagram on paper. It will save you time in the long run, and help you to avoid costly errors.

Notes

You're halfway there:

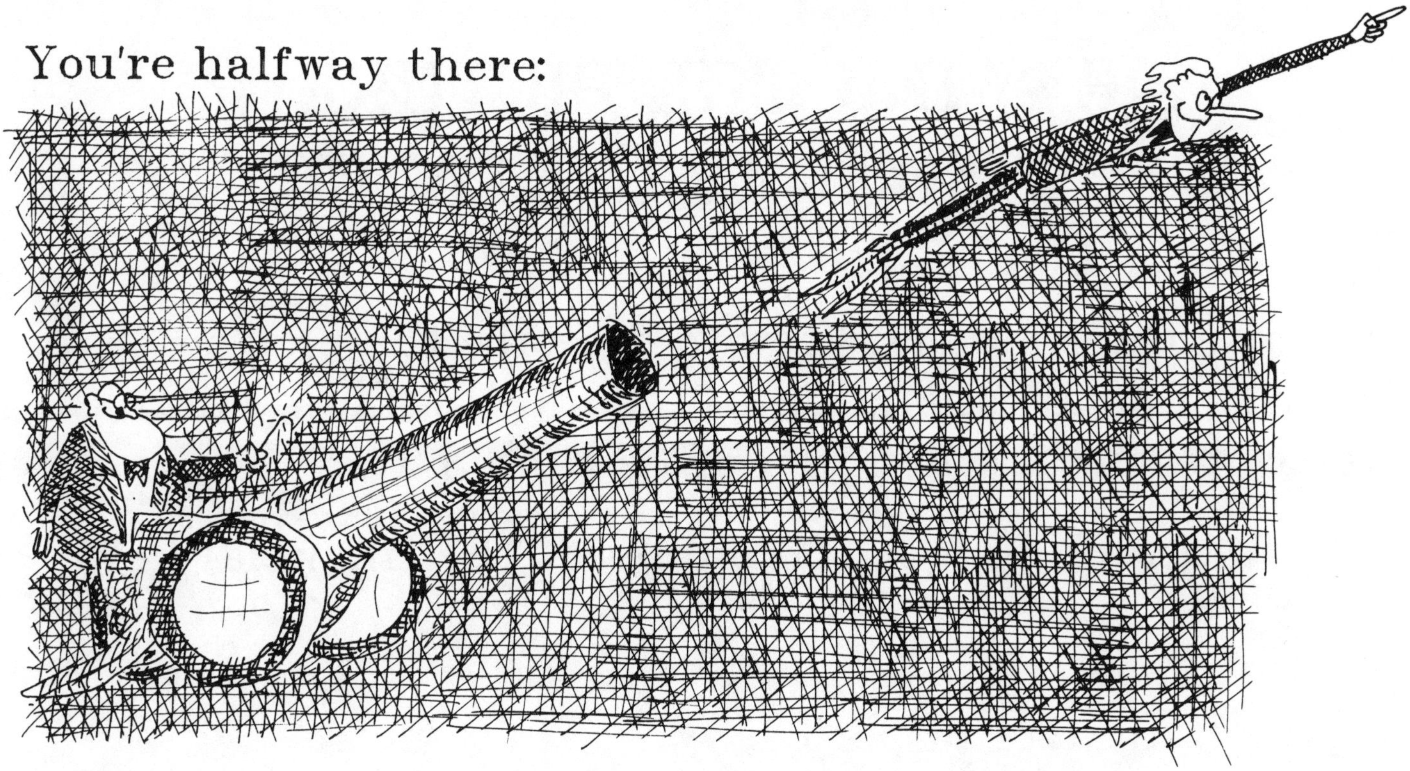

1. You know how to define a problem clearly.

2. Now you need to be able to present the right question to your calculator--in terms it will understand.

Your calculator can't see that nice cash-flow diagram you draw for yourself. You have to describe that picture for it.

You gotta speak the language....

DRAWING THE PICTURE FOR YOUR CALCULATOR

You use the financial keys to describe the picture to your financial calculator, so it's nice to know what you're telling it when you press those keys.

As you saw on page 9, the names of the financial keys are:

[n]	number of periods
[i]	interest rate
[PV]	Present Value
[PMT]	Payment
[FV]	Future Value

The best way to think about these keys is that they form a picture frame that you can set over a cash–flow diagram:

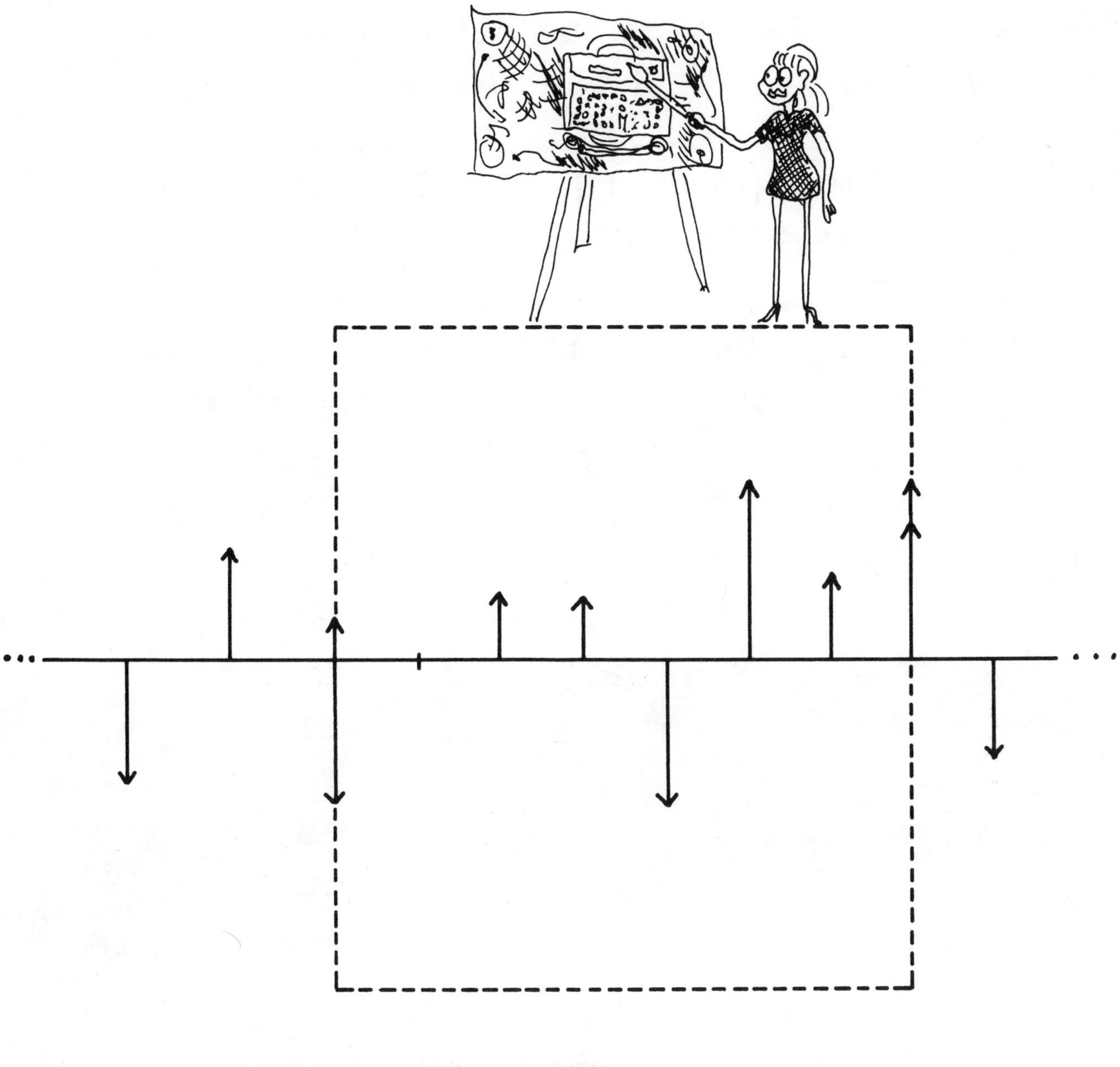

PV, FV, n, and PMT

The Present Value (PV) is the net cash–flow that occurs at the left side of the picture.

The Future Value (FV) is the net cash–flow that occurs at the right side of the picture.

The number of periods (n) is just that––it's the number of D.I.P.'s occurring between the PV and the FV.

The payment (PMT) is a convenience item, really, for cases where the picture is like this:

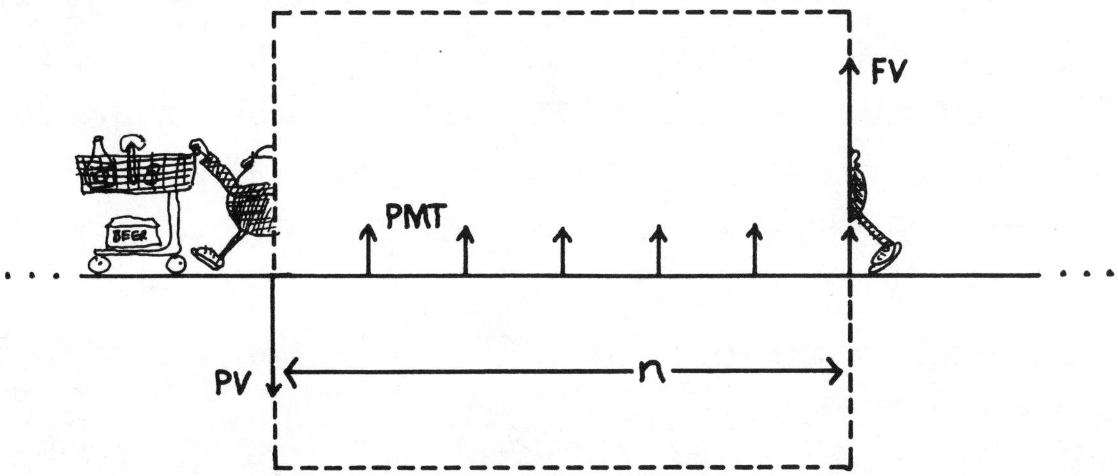

The payment amount is the amount of EACH of a level series of cash–flows––each occurring exactly once every D.I.P. That means there are "n" PMT's.

On the above diagram, n = 6, so there are six payments.

Now, when you store numbers in the PV–, PMT–, and FV–registers, you're telling the calculator the amounts of these cash–flows and their directions (up or down). You indicate direction by adjusting the sign (positive or negative) of these numbers. Use positive numbers for the upward cash–flows (when you receive money). Use negative numbers for the downward cash–flows (when you pay money).

Remember how to use the [CHS] key? (If not, see page 25.)

Another thing: The HP–12C demands that PV and FV be of opposite sign. If PV is negative, then FV must be positive, and vice versa.

This is consistent with the idea of investment and return (or borrowing and repayment), right?

(Right.)

Here's another look at that loan picture you just saw:

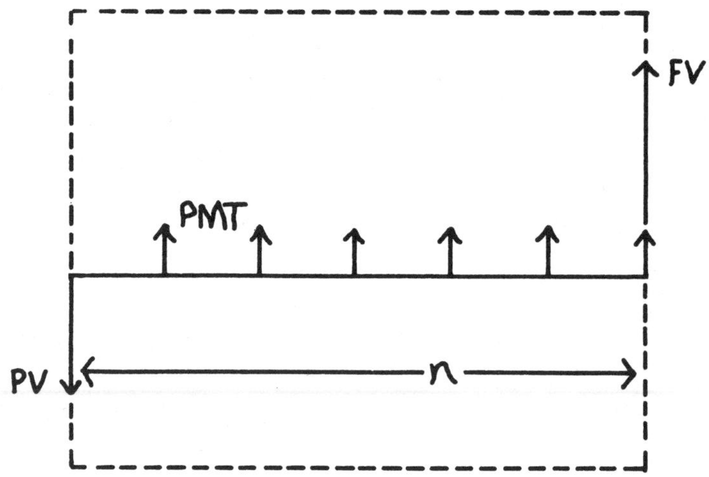

Wondering why there are two arrows at the right-hand end? After all, you could "net" them into one transaction, couldn't you?

The reason is this:

FV is the cash-flow that occurs at the right end of the picture frame OVER AND ABOVE the PMT that may occur there (even if the two occur simultaneously).

And PV is the left-side cash-flow OVER and ABOVE any PMT that may occur there.

That's what the calculator means by PV and FV.

i

You've probably noticed that nothing's been said about the i key yet. It's really very simple:

The number in the i–register represents the Defined Interest Rate (D.I.R.) in percentage form. It's the rate that corresponds to the Defined Interest Period (D.I.P.). (D.I.R. and D.I.P. are discussed back on page 80. If you've forgotten what they mean, review them now.)

"So how does this fit into the picture frame idea?"

The interest is the "glue" that holds that frame together. In effect, it determines how big FV must be to compensate for PV and for "n" periods of PMT's.

ATTENTION!
THIS IS VERY IMPORTANT!!

The numbers n, i, and PMT are all concerned with the same time period, namely, the Defined Interest Period (D.I.P).

If the D.I.P. is monthly, you can't use an annual interest rate and expect to get the right answer.

If the D.I.P. is daily, so is the D.I.R.

If the D.I.P. is quarterly, then again, you have to match the rate to the period.

If this seems like preaching, that's good. You won't forget:

ALWAYS MAKE SURE THAT [n], [i], AND [PMT]
ARE ALL DEALING WITH THE SAME TIME PERIOD.

Now you're all set:

A. You know how to picture the "insides" of your calculator, how to use it to do arithmetic, and how to use the keyboard.

B. You know how to use cash–flow diagrams to define a problem and you know that it's "legal" to move cash–flows around on that timeline.

C. You know what you're telling the calculator when you put numbers into the 5 FINANCIAL registers.

But you haven't had any "hands–on" experience...yet.

And by now all this information is probably floating around in a financial fog in your mind....

Yes...it's that time!

FINANCIAL CALCULATIONS

Here's a good first example. Now all this fog will start making some sense.

You want to borrow $6000.00 to buy a car. You want a 48–month loan with regular monthly payments that completely pays off the loan in those 48 installments.

The current interest rate is 13.5% A.P.R.

What will your monthly payment be?

If you know how to solve this, try page 114.

But if you're in the slightest doubt....

That was a fairly complete description of a typical loan problem. But one detail is missing:

Will the monthly payments be made at the beginning **or at the end of each month?**

Does it even make a difference?

Well, compare the two pictures:

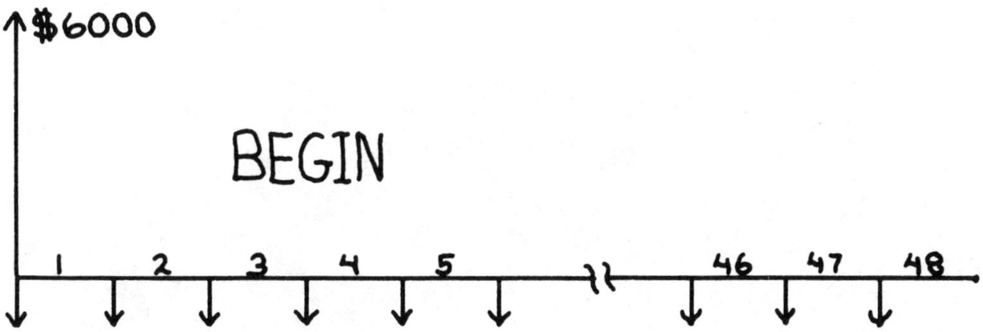

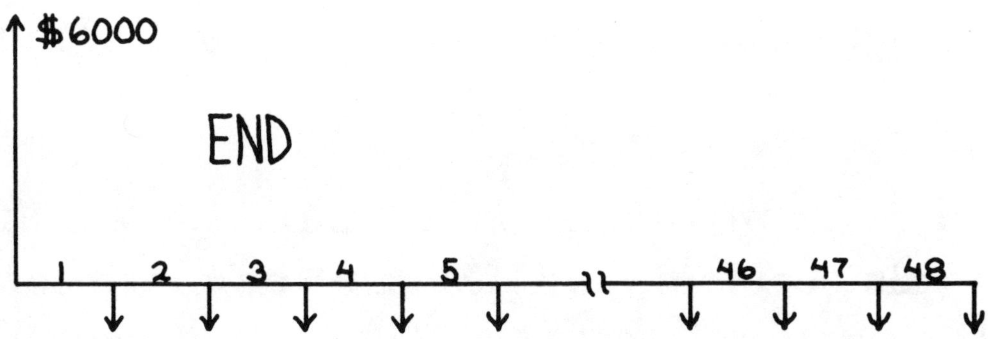

BEGIN OR END?

As you can see, in the first case, a payment is due at the beginning of the loan. This reduces the balance sooner, so there is less interest paid on the borrowed money.

With less interest to be paid, the PMT amount (which covers both interest and principal) will be less.

So, it DOES matter whether the payment is at the BEGinning or the END of the period.

So what about your car loan? Which is it going to be?

Well, in a real contract, it would have to be stated, **but for this problem, just assume the more common** case—the payment occurs at the END of each month.

Notice that your calculator has two operations called BEGIN [BEG] and END [END]. These operations do nothing but tell the calculator whether the payment will occur at the beginning or end of the period.

See the blue–printed BEG and END?

If you press [g] [BEG], you'll put the machine into BEGIN mode. Try it. Notice the little BEGIN that appears in the display to remind you what "annuity mode" is selected. (Did you like how that word "annuity" sneaked in there?)

Now press [g] [END]. The BEGIN annunciator disappears. The machine is in END mode. That is what you want for your car loan.

Next, since you've established the correct annuity mode, you should draw the cash–flow diagram that is correct for your perspective.

DRAW THE PICTURE

(This isn't too hard––you've already seen it.)

You're the borrower, so you receive the loan and pay the installments; when you key in your PV, it will be positive, and the PMT amount you calculate should come out negative:

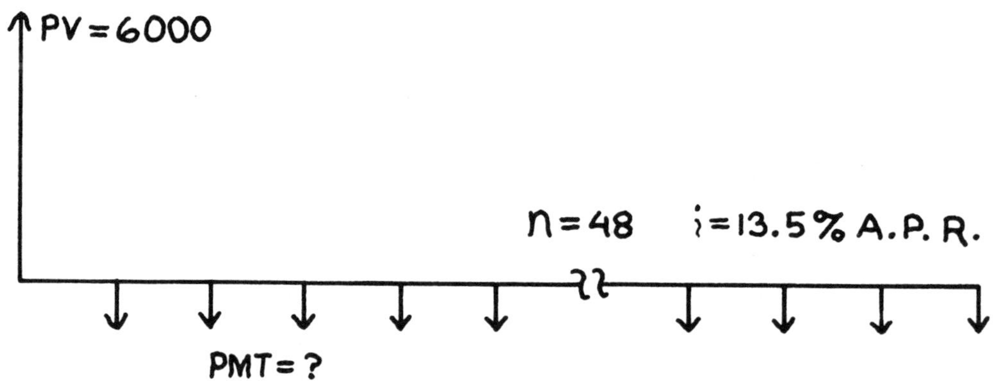

The unknown on this diagram is the PMT. You want to find what your payments will be.

What about FV? What is it?

In this case, there is no FV; that is, FV = 0. The description of the loan said it would be entirely paid off (amortized) by those 48 level payments.

Remember what FV represents? It's the amount of the remaining transaction AFTER the 48th month and AFTER the 48th payment. If there's nothing left, then FV must be zero.

But you still need to tell that to the calculator! Don't just assume that the FV-register contains a zero.

Remember! That "C" in "HP–12C" means Continuous memory. If there's some non–zero number in any register, it will stay there for months––until you change it. It's like a budget deficit. It won't just melt into zero because you ignore it.

FOR EVERY CALCULATION YOU PERFORM WITH THE FINANCIAL REGISTERS, YOU SHOULD USE FOUR NUMBERS TO SOLVE FOR THE FIFTH.
NEVER IGNORE ONE!

So, you've pretty well defined the problem...

END mode
PV = 6000
FV = 0
n = 48
PMT is the unknown you're after.

Wait a minute. What's i?

The interest rate was quoted as 13.5% A.P.R., but it doesn't say how often compounding occurs.

The fact is, there are many times when the only clue you have is the payment period. If the payment period is monthly, then unless it's stated otherwise, the interest will compound monthly.

You have to translate that 13.5% A.P.R. (Annual Percentage Rate) into a monthly D.I.R. (Defined Interest Rate).

Unless it's specifically stated otherwise, an A.P.R. is usually a nominal quote. This means it's only a convenient approximation of reality.

The number 13.5% is the actual monthly D.I.R. multiplied by 12.

The effective annual rate of interest is higher than 13.5% because of the compound nature of monthly interest, but calculation of this percentage rate is more complicated. They didn't have HP–12C's back then, so the A.P.R. has become a convention and convenience.

Try this: Convert this 13.5% nominal A.P.R. to the monthly D.I.R.

Solution: 13.5 [ENTER] 12 [÷]   Answer: 1.125

Now store this answer in the i-register--press [i].

Plug in the other values you know:

[g] [END]	(already set)
6000 [PV]	(If you think about what's happening in the financial registers, you'll realize that the order in which you key in these values doesn't matter.)
0 [FV]	
48 [n]	

Now solve for the payment by pressing [PMT]. The answer is –162.46. It's negative because you're paying it, not receiving it.

TO REVIEW

1. You got a verbal description of the loan.

2. You decided on the annuity mode: END mode (also called "annuity in arrears").

3. You drew the correct picture of the situation on a cash–flow diagram, establishing your perspective as a borrower and therefore the signs (+ or –) of PV, PMT, and FV.

4. You observed that since the 48 payments completely "amortized" the loan, FV must be zero.

5. You computed the correct Defined Interest Rate from the quoted nominal A.P.R. and stored it in [i].

6. You "plugged in" all the other information––PV = 6000, n = 48, FV = 0, END mode––and solved for PMT.

Cake, right?

But keep in mind that you're learning more than just this example. Retain the concepts––don't just concentrate on a given set of keystrokes!

After all, the keystroke procedure itself is pretty trivial, right? The difficult part is deciding what to put into the calculator so that it will grind out the correct answer.

$162.46

There's your car payment, OK?...

...what's that? You say you can't afford that much every month?

Well, how much can you pay?

$125.00?

Fine, but that means there will be a lump–sum remaining balance at the end of 48 months. At this interest rate, $125 per month simply won't amortize $6000 in 48 payments. (It takes $162.46 per month to do that, as you just proved.)

Are you willing to pay that "balloon payment," as it's called?

Better figure out how much it will be.

(If you already know how to do this, then do it and skip ahead to page 119.)

First, better see what this looks like on a cash–flow diagram:

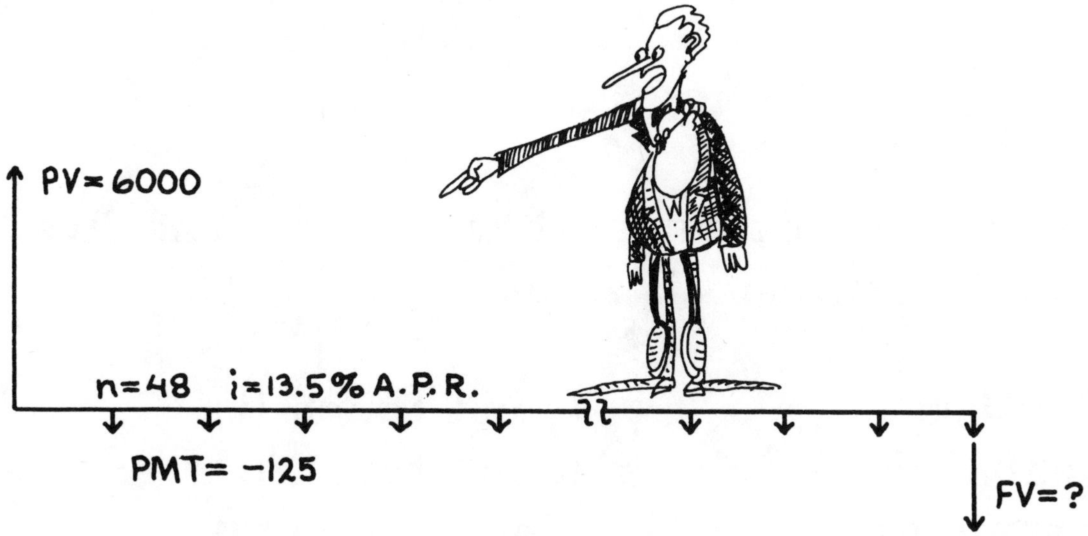

This time, you know the payment amount (PMT). It's $125.00, and from your perspective, the payment is a downward arrow, right?

But you don't know FV. That's the balloon amount ––the balance remaining AFTER the 48th PMT and AFTER the 48th D.I.P. (Remember this definition? It's on page 101.)

This is a good example where none of the five financial numbers is zero.

PV = 6000	(don't touch it)
n = 48	(don't touch it)
i = same as before	(don't touch it)
PMT = –125	

The only thing you're changing is PMT. FV will be calculated from the above information, so don't waste your time keying everything in again. Just change the one number:

125 [CHS] [PMT].

Now find the balloon payment: [FV] -----> –2366.81

(Whew! You'll have to pay $2366.81 at the end of 48 months.)

Starting to get the idea? Here's how the FINANCIAL–registers look at this point:

Financial Registers

Uh–oh!...you say the balloon amount is too steep? (Sigh.) All right...better find a happy medium. What's the greatest balloon amount you'd tolerate?

$1000.00?

Fine. Now check to see what PMT amount that implies:

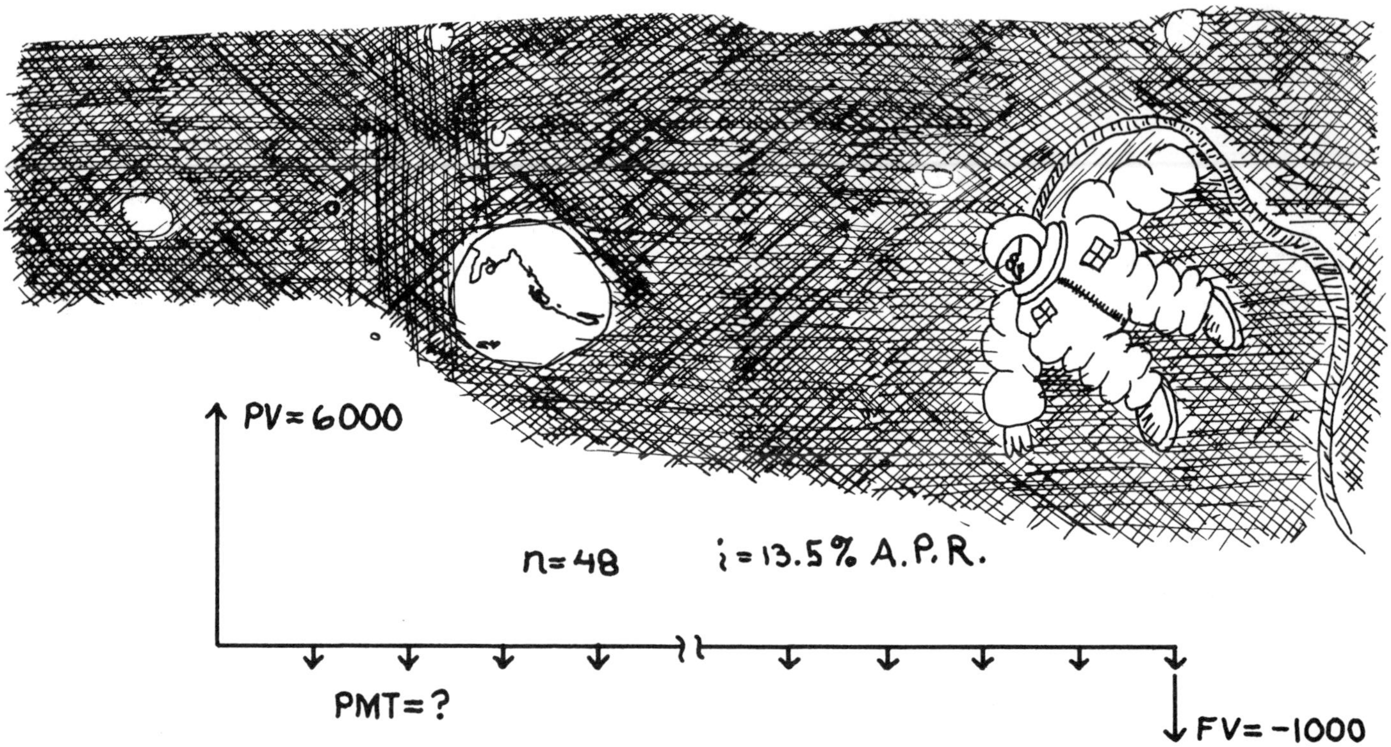

Change only what you have to:

1000 [CHS] [FV]

Then find the corresponding payment.

Press [PMT]. Answer: –146.63

Is that payment OK (relatively speaking)...? It is?

("Hey, we have a winner!")

You should be getting comfortable with the idea of playing "what-if?" with the different loan parameters: you change one parameter at a time, leave 3 others intact, and solve for the fifth.

Need some more practice?

Well, you're going to get it, because now that you've decided what loan you can afford, you have to find a lender who will agree to it.

(No rest for the weary.)

The first lender agrees to all the specifics of your loan--except one:

It turns out that the interest rate is a nominal 13.5%, all right, but it's compounded DAILY. What does that do to your loan?

How do you compute a monthly payment with daily compounding interest? The D.I.P. (Defined Interest Period) doesn't match the payment period. (If you already know how to get around this, turn to page 126.)

As you know, the payment period and the interest period must ALWAYS match if you want to get the right answer with your calculator.

So it boils down to this: You need to convert a daily compounding rate to its equivalent monthly compounding rate.

That is, you're going to declare that the D.I.P. is one month, instead of one day. But of course, that means you also have to redefine the D.I.R. to a matching monthly rate. (It's a preliminary calculation you have to do before recalculating your payment or balloon.)

Now, if one D.I.R. is truly equivalent to another, both rates must produce an identical amount of interest on the dollar in any given time period, right?

OK, pick a convenient dollar amount, $100.00, and a convenient time period, 1 year. Use these convenient numbers to calculate a monthly D.I.R. from the given daily D.I.R.

If 13.5% is compounded daily, then this daily D.I.R. is:

$$(13.5 \div 365)\%$$

(Some banks use 360 days in a year, but you can assume 365 for this one.)

Put that percentage into the i–register:

13.5 ENTER 365 ÷ i

Now, if $100 accrues for 1 year at that interest rate (compounded daily), how much will you have?

365 n	(There are 365 days in a year.)
100 PV	(That's the starting amount in this little experiment.)
0 PMT	(You add nothing during the year.)

The balance after 1 year will be (press FV).

–114.45

You've just computed the amount that $100 would grow to if you left it for a year in an account at 13.5%, compounded daily.

Next, you want to know what rate--compounded monthly--will do the same thing to that $100.

The present value [PV] is still 100, the future value [FV] is still −114.45, and there's no payment. Don't touch these keys.

You want to calculate an interest rate ([i]) for 12 periods. So:

12 [n]
[i] Answer: 1.1311 (Remember how to use [f] 4 ?)

That must be your effective monthly rate, which is entirely equivalent to 13.5% A.P.R. compounded daily. This is your new D.I.R.

Now, since you have the correct monthly rate sitting in the i–register, leave it there.

And go back to the original question: What does this rate do to your car loan payment, assuming you'll tolerate a balloon amount of $1000?

Here's the picture again:

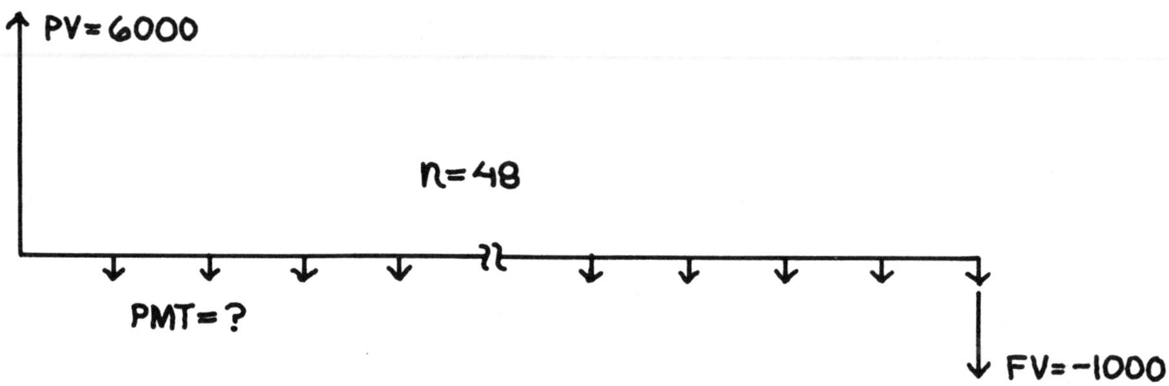

Plug it in (make sure END mode is set):

48 [n]
Don't touch [i]
6000 [PV]
1000 [CHS] [FV]
[PMT]   Answer: –146.88

Well, that doesn't change it much--only a twenty-five cent increase (over the original payment amount you figured, $146.63). But now that you've had a taste of "wheeling and dealing," you decide to shop around for a better deal on your wheels. So, armed with an HP-12C, you head to the next prospect.

On the way, of course, you're thinking about how that daily compounding can jack up the effective rate. By compounding more often, small amounts of interest are added on earlier, so that each small amount is there to collect interest sooner. It boggles the mind, but it works.

With a slightly boggled mind, you turn to the problem at hand...

The next firm down the road will agree to most of your terms, including monthly compounding (13.5%), but they throw in this added stipulation:

A finance charge equal to 1% of the loan must be paid at the time the loan is signed.

This charge does NOT reduce the repayment amount; it's a separate fee altogether.

How does this look?

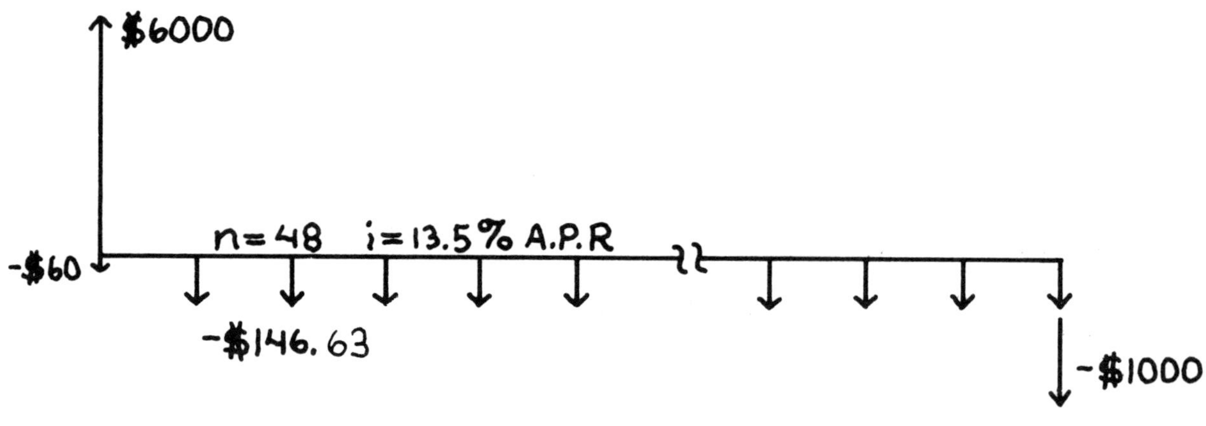

Obviously, it's not as good a deal as the straightforward loan you want. With the finance charge, you're simply paying more money.

Look at the picture. Remember the rule? When two or more cash–flows occur simultaneously, you can add them together to get one net cash–flow.

You receive a $6000 loan, but at the same time, you pay a $60 finance charge. You're really receiving a $5940 loan. BUT, you're still making payments on the full $6000. That finance charge is NOT applied toward the balance.

What does this do to the interest rate you're being charged? Is the nominal rate still 13.5%?

(If you know how to solve this, try page 131.)

Of course, your payment and balloon will be just what you prescribed (recompute it here for practice):

([g] [END])
48 [n]
6000 [PV]
13.5 [ENTER] 12 [÷] [i]
1000 [CHS] [FV]
[PMT] Answer: −146.63 Look familiar?

That's what you'll pay every month. But the amount you receive is only $5940.00.

What's the true A.P.R. you're paying? What interest rate is the "glue" holding this picture together?

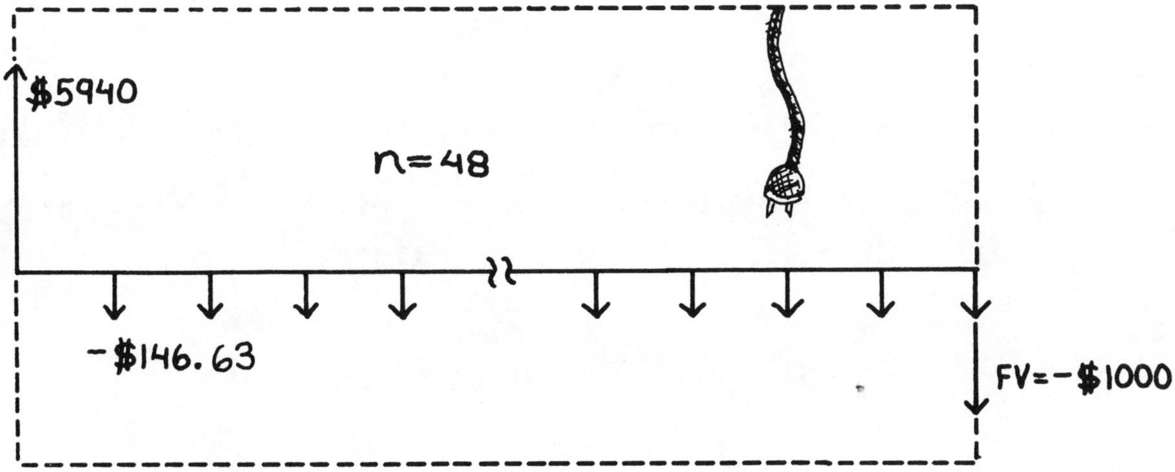

Well, just plug in the new present value:

5940 [PV]

And solve for i. (Don't touch the other keys.)

[i]   Answer: 1.1660

That's a monthly rate, because the D.I.P. is one month. To convert to a nominal A.P.R., just multiply by 12:

12 [X] Answer: 13.99

Wow! That's not the 13.5% you were looking for, is it?

See how "points up front"--those prepaid finance charges--can change the true interest on a loan? So, you don't go for that one either?

OK...you try a third lender....

These folks are more helpful. They'll go for the loan as prescribed except they would like each payment at the beginning of the month, rather than at the end ("annuity in advance," instead of "annuity in arrears").

How does this change things?

Well, you've already seen the two pictures compared. (Look back at page 106.)

If you agree to this loan, you'll owe a payment immediately upon signing. This starts to sound like a finance charge, but it's not. In this case, the initial payment DOES apply toward repaying the loan.

And this DOES change the PMT amount:

[g] [BEG] (annuity in advance)
6000 [PV]
48 [n]
13.5 [ENTER] 12 [÷] [i]
1000 [CHS] [FV]
[PMT] Answer: –145.00 (Why is it negative?)

That's LOWER (and a nice even number)!

You'll take it?

Great. It looks like that car is practically yours ...(heh, heh)...

Hold on a minute! There seems to be a little hocus–pocus going on here!

YOU will save money, and the lender will earn a true–green 13.5% A.P.R. (compounded monthly)!

Voodoo economics?

No, there's no contradiction here. You'll save money, not by paying a lower interest rate, but by borrowing for a SHORTER TIME (i.e. because of BEGin mode, you're paying back the money sooner). The same rate will, of course, earn different dollar amounts over different lengths of time.

So:

1. The lender is happy with the earnings.
2. The car dealer is happy with the sale.
3. You're happy with the car and satisfied with the loan.

But, are you satisfied with your understanding of the 5 financial keys on your HP–12C?

Now you should be able to solve these types of problems:

1. A loan with no balloon payment.

2. A loan with a balloon payment.

3. A conversion from a daily compounding rate to the equivalent monthly rate (matching the D.I.P. to the payment period).

4. A loan with prepaid finance charges ("points up front").

5. A loan in BEGIN mode.

SO....

TEST YOURSELF

Solve these problems. In case you need hints, the solutions are on the following pages. Remember, a cash–flow diagram is a must!

1. A mortgage is written at 15.5% A.P.R. It amortizes totally in 30 years of $400 monthly payments (in arrears). What is the loan amount?

2. If the above loan had $350.00 payments (annuity in advance), what would the remaining balance be after the 360th month? After the 120th month?

3. A finance company agrees to loan $100,000.00 at 17% A.P.R., compounded daily (on a 360–day year), in exchange for quarterly payments (in arrears) that will amortize the loan in 15 years. A 2% finance charge is due and payable at the beginning of the loan. (Good grief!)

   a. **What is the payment amount?**

   b. **What is the remaining balance after 10 years?**

   c. **What is the nominal A.P.R. earned for that 10 year situation (considering the "points up front")?**

   d. **What EFFECTIVE annual interest does that nominal A.P.R. represent?**

4. Suppose you had arranged your car loan like this (annuity in arrears):

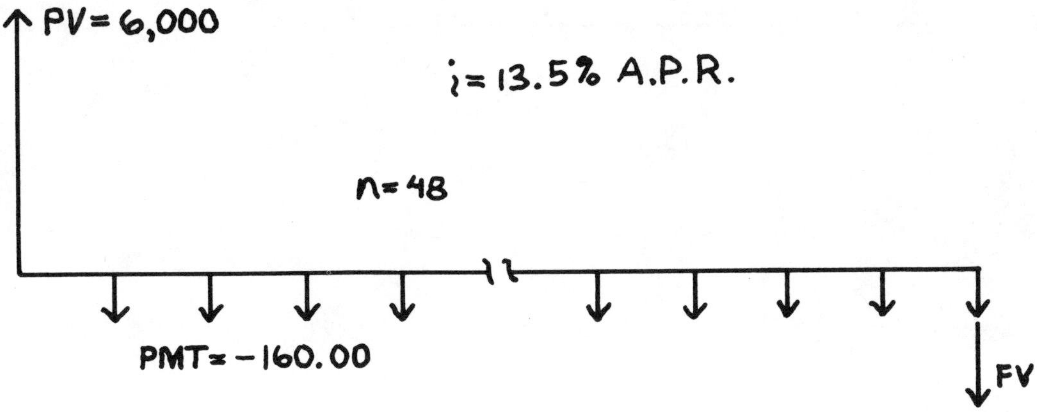

You make 17 payments as prescribed, but at the end of the 18th month, you decide to pay off $2500.00 (of principal and interest) in one lump sum.

Then you decide not to make payments for 10 months. At the end of that 28th month, the lender claims that the remaining balance is $2041.94. Is this correct?

TEST SOLUTIONS

1. The situation is this:

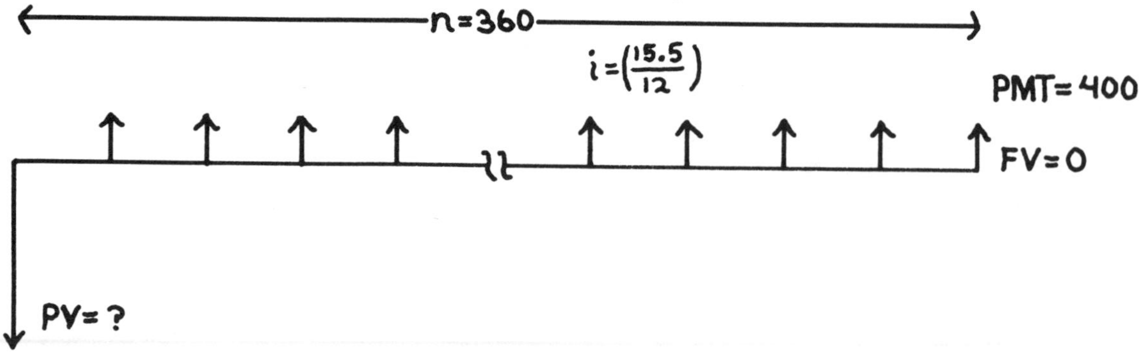

g END

360 n

15.5 ENTER 12 ÷ i

400 PMT 0 FV

Solve for the present value: PV Answer: –30,662.69

This was the amount of the mortgage. (Sort of a weird number for a mortgage.) This problem was solved from the perspective of the lender. (How do you know this? See page 87, if you don't remember.)

(These stack diagrams show the fact that when you use the financial keys storage shortcut, the stack is left disabled. For instance, after you store 360 in the n–register, that 360 doesn't get pushed up into the stack when you key in 15.5. Keep this in mind.)

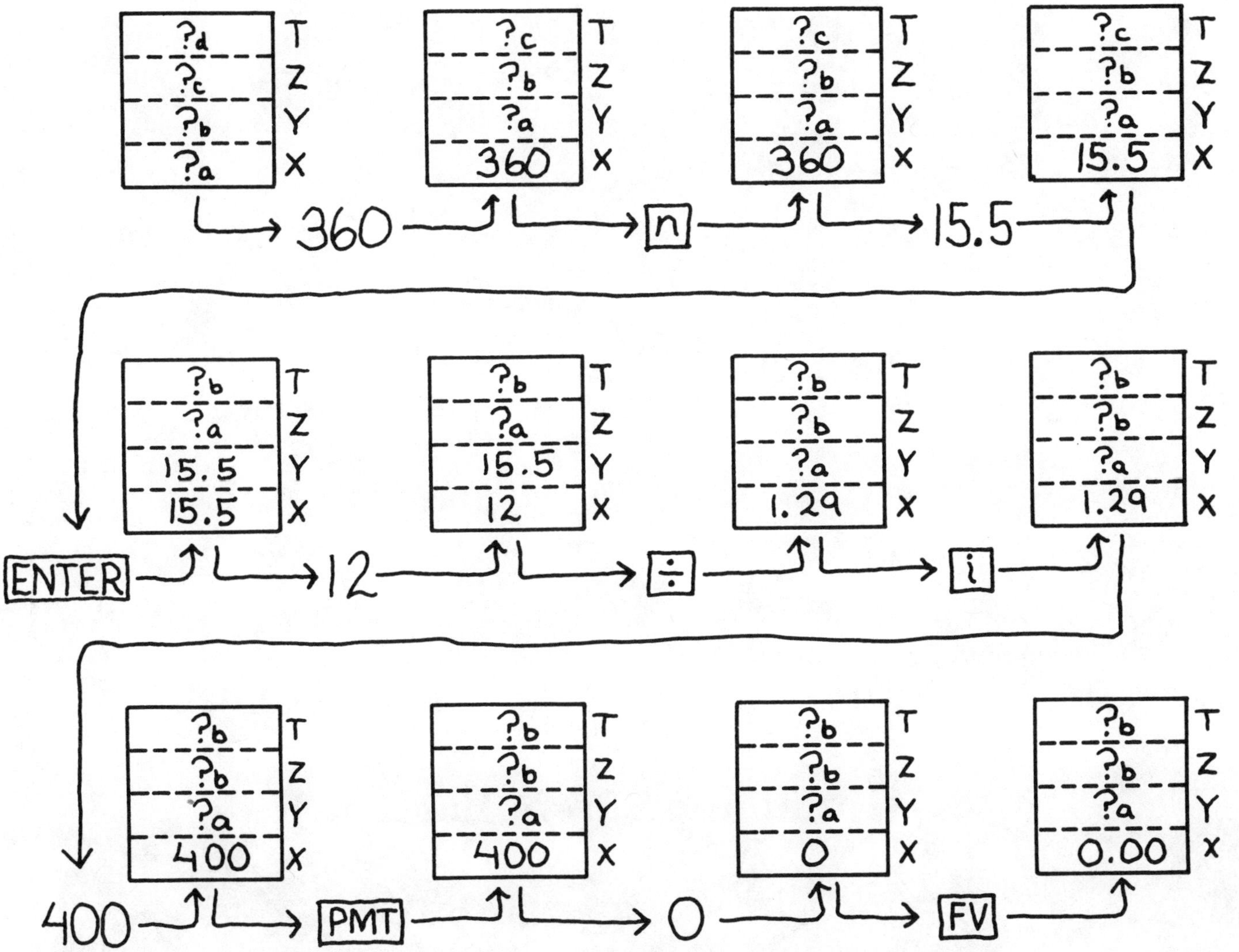

2. The new situation is this:

(360–month balloon)

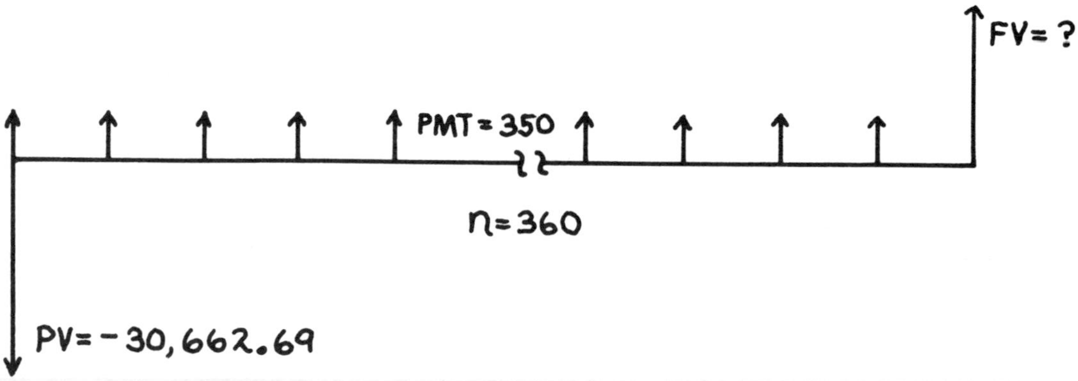

Don't touch [n], [PV], or [i]; they're all correct.
Just press:

[g] [BEG]
350 [PMT]

Solve for the future value: [FV] Answer: 353,916.61

("...Holy jumpnupndown, Martha!")

That balloon is over 10 times the original amount of the loan! How can this be?

Well, in this case, the payments are too small. The interest charged each month is more than the payment, so the future value INCREASES every month.

Now look at the 120–month balloon:

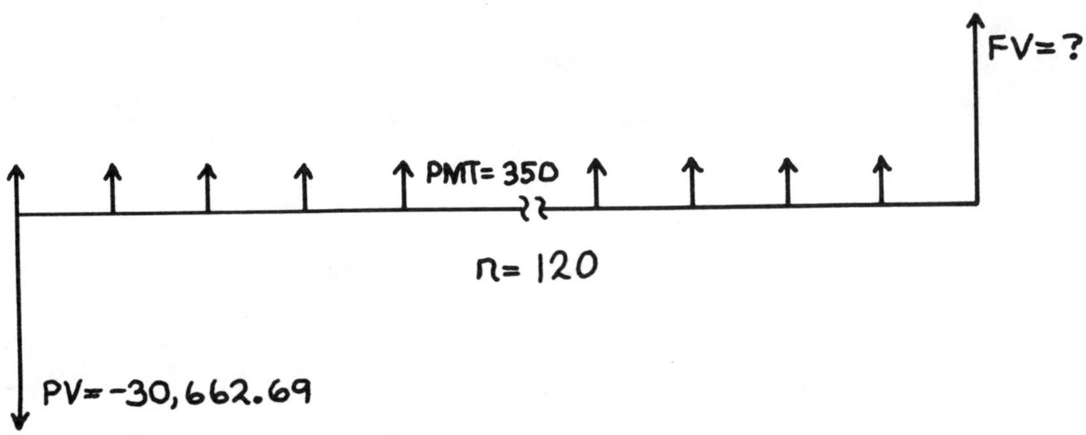

Solution: 120 [n] [FV]   Answer: 42,448.84

3. Here's the initial situation:

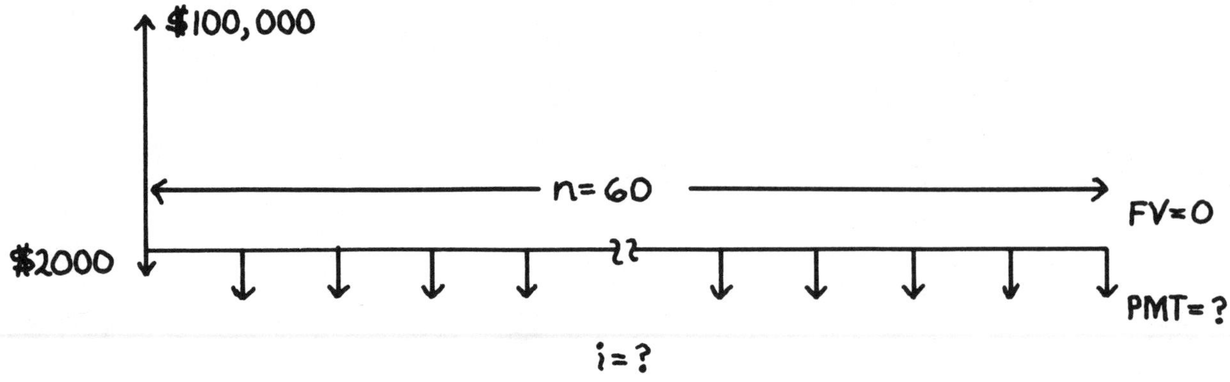

First, find i by converting the daily rate to a quarterly rate:

[g] [END]
17 [ENTER] 360 [n] [÷] [i]
100 [PV] (Pick this amount for convenience.)
0 [PMT] (Let it grow at 17% compounded daily.)
[FV] (gives –118.53)

4 [n] (four periods in quarterly compounding.)
[i] Answer: 4.3406

(That's the new D.I.R. for quarterly compounding. Leave it in the i–register.)

Now find the payment for this loan situation.

100,000 [PV]
60 [n] (15 years has 60 quarters)
(Don't touch [i])
0 [FV] (Why zero? See page 110.)
[PMT] Answer: −4708.42

(Voila!)

Next, find the remaining balance after 10 years (40 payments):

40 [n] [FV] Answer: −62,101.87

Now, considering the "points–up–front" finance charge, the actual nominal A.P.R. is easy to calculate:

98,000 [PV] (Why is this 2% less? See pages 131–132, if you don't know.)
[i] (4.4589 is a quarterly rate)
4 [X] Answer: 17.84%

Next, you're asked to turn this nominal rate into an effective annual rate: "What really happens to $100 in 4 quarters at this quarterly compounded rate?"

4 [n]
100 [CHS] [PV]
0 [PMT] [FV] (gives the year–end balance)
[RCL] [PV] [+] 19.06 is the interest earned, and since it was earned on $100, it is also the effective percentage. Pretty slick, eh?

---

4. The cash–flow diagram looks like this:

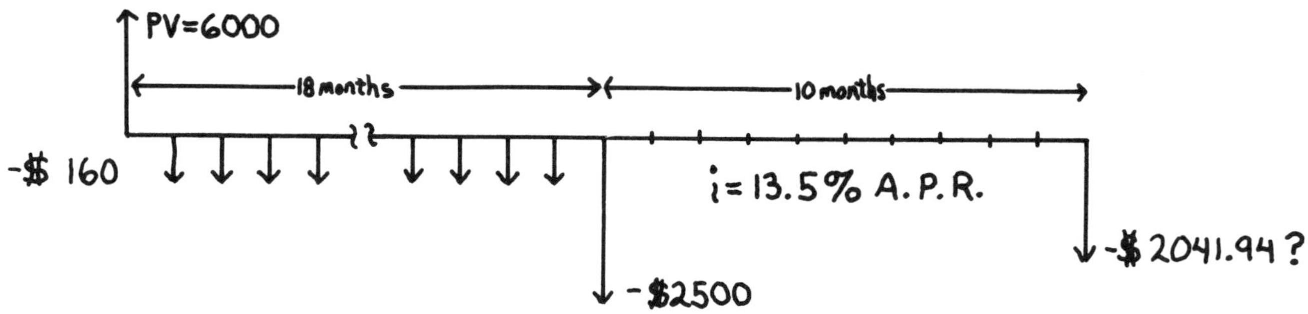

This problem needs to be solved in two parts:

PART ONE:

First, put the picture frame over those first 18 months:

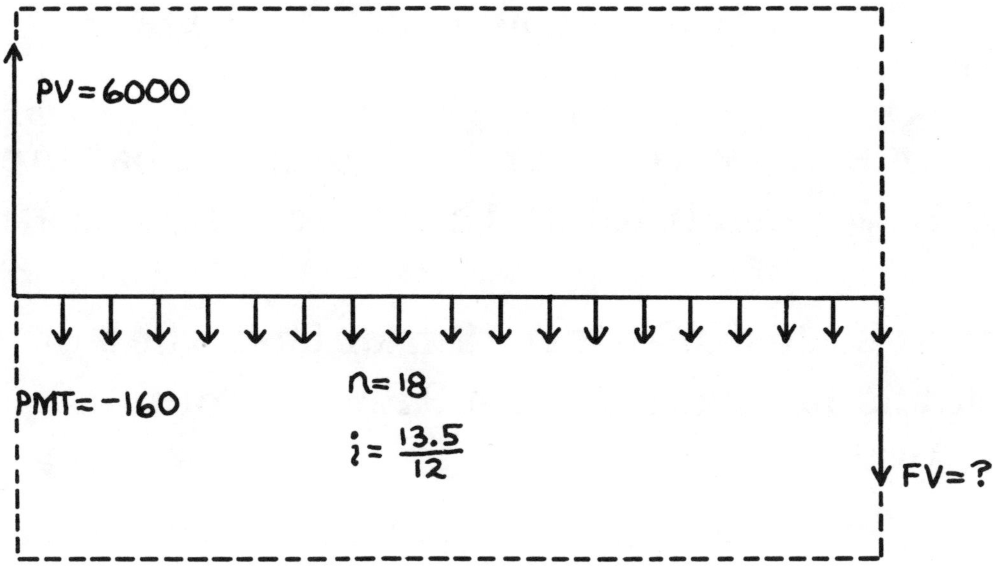

FV represents, as always, the remaining balance.

18 [n]

13.5 [ENTER] 12 [÷] [i]

6000 [PV]

160 [CHS] [PMT]

[FV] Answer: −4,165.82

That's what you would owe after the 18th regular payment. But you paid an 18th payment of $2500, which is $2340 more than a regular installment required.

PART TWO:

So you've reduced this $4,165.82 by an additional $2340.

(4165.82–2340.00 = 1825.82)

So the true balance after that balloon payment is $1825.82. Wonderful...but that's not the question.

If you owe $1825.82 after 18 months, what do you owe 10 months later (at 13.5% A.P.R. compounded monthly)?

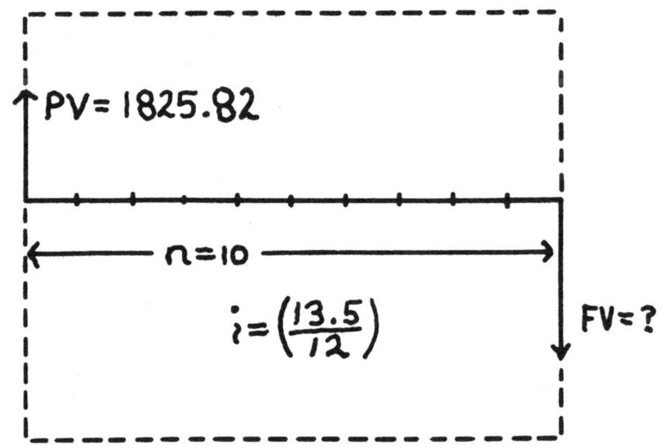

The picture frame is now set over months 19 through 28. It's exactly like a new loan where you owe $1825.82 at the beginning. Now the procedure is trivial:

[RCL] [FV] [CHS] 2340 [–] [PV]
10 [n]
0 [PMT]
[FV] Answer: –2041.94 The lender is right (sigh).

"I say, that last problem (number 4) was a bit tricky! Once it was broken into two parts, it was a little easier, true, but there's got to be a better way to approach this!"

Well, there is, but first you have to learn some new concepts. So set your calculator down for a few pages while you learn about...

UNEVEN CASH FLOWS.

The thing that makes problem 4 so difficult is the UNEVEN cash–flows.

The final payment schedule that you and the lender agreed upon looks like this (these are only the payments):

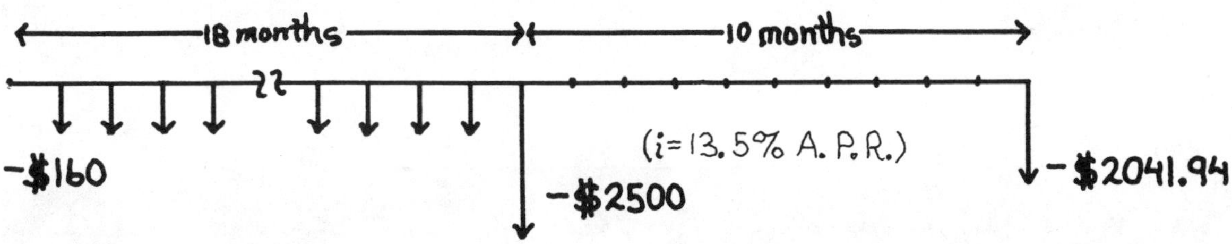

Because those payments aren't all identical, you had to break the problem into two parts in order to use the 5–key solution (n, i, PV, PMT, FV), because the PMT key demands identical payments.

There's another key that doesn't care if those cash–flows are even or not....

NET PRESENT VALUE (NPV)

Here's that payment schedule again:

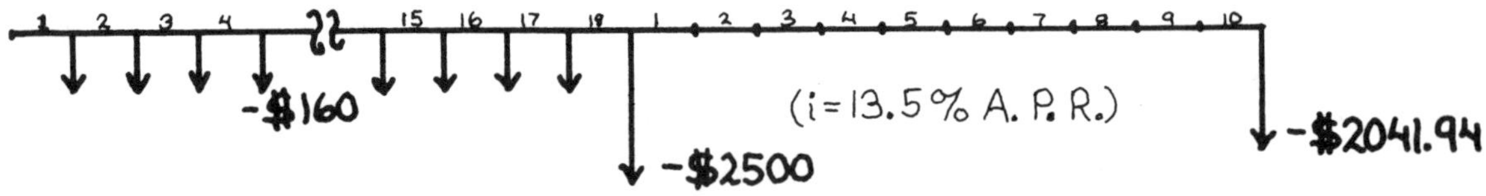

Now, the lender claims that if the prevailing interest rate is 13.5% A.P.R., this payment schedule has a "value" (up front) of $6000.00. In other words, if you agree to embark upon this schedule of payments, the lender will give you $6000 now, and that $6000 will be earning 13.5% A.P.R. for the lender.

"Yes, that's what I was trying to prove in problem 4, right?"

Right. And wouldn't it be nice if you could prove this in one step on the HP–12C? Wouldn't it be nice if you could easily obtain this one lump sum that represents the true NET PRESENT VALUE of that payment schedule?

Nothing Is Impossible.

You've already seen cases of sliding cash–flows up and down the time line, but look again––closely––at this process.

In this cash–flow situation (from problem 4);

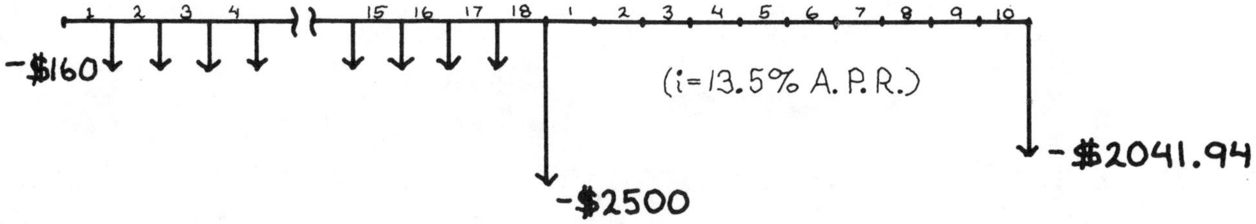

if you were to slide the first $160.00 payment to the beginning of the time line, it would look like this:

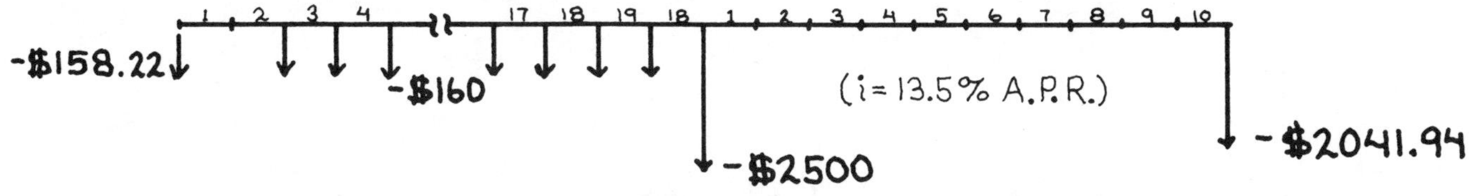

By sliding it back one month, the first $160 payment is reduced (by the 13.5% A.P.R) to $158.22. (Don't worry about confirming this number, but understand why it gets reduced. Look back on page 90, if you don't understand.)

Next if you were to slide the second payment back, it would look like this:

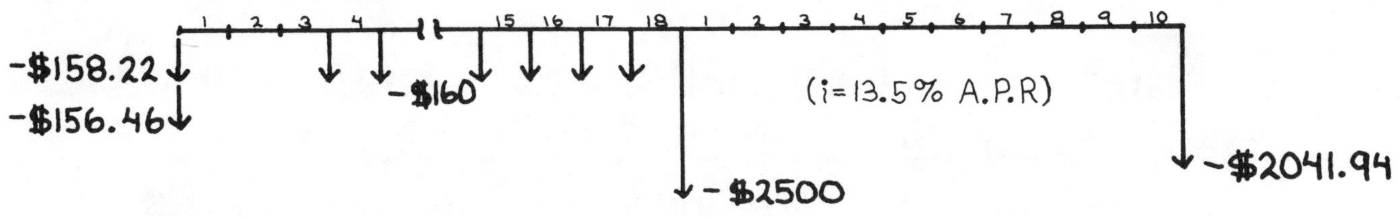

The second $160 payment is reduced to $156.46 by sliding it back 2 months.

If you were to continue in this endeavor...

Slide back the third payment:

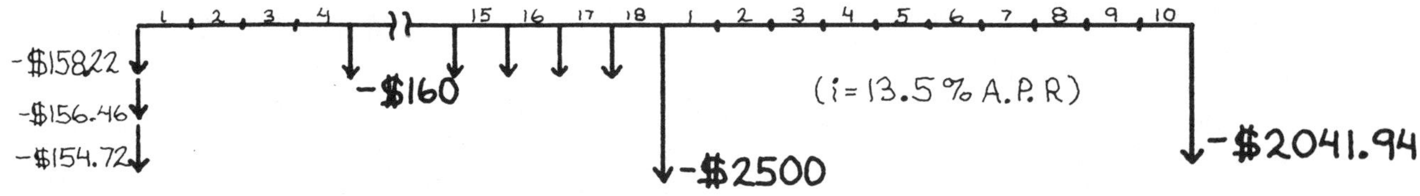

Slide back the fourth payment:

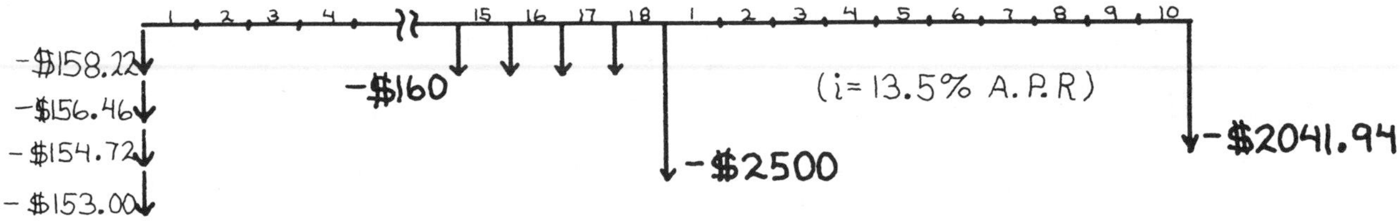

Etc.

And keep sliding cash–flows back to the beginning of the time line (even the $2500 cash–flow and the $2041.94 cash–flow) and finally add up (i.e. "net") all those cash–flows at the beginning of the time line, you would end up with this:

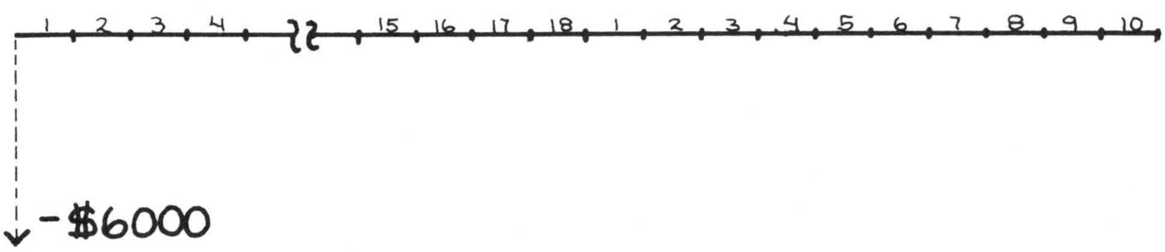

This is said to be the NET PRESENT VALUE of that payment schedule. And, because ALL of those cash–flows were negative, the net present value of those cash–flows is also negative (the arrow is pointing down).

So, if the lender's claim is correct (as it was already proven to be in the solution of problem 4, page 145), then this cash–flow situation,

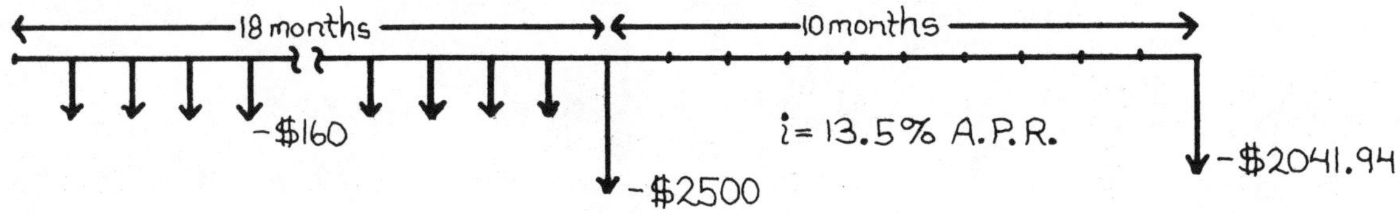

has a Net Present Value of –$6000.00.

To summarize, the Net Present Value of a cash–flow diagram is the number that results when you sum up all the cash–flows on that diagram AFTER HAVING SLID EACH CASH–FLOW TO THE BEGINNING OF THE TIME LINE (ADJUSTING EACH ACCORDING TO THE PREVAILING INTEREST RATE). It's simple, right...?

TEST

(No calculators allowed)

1. What is the Net present value of this cash–flow situation?

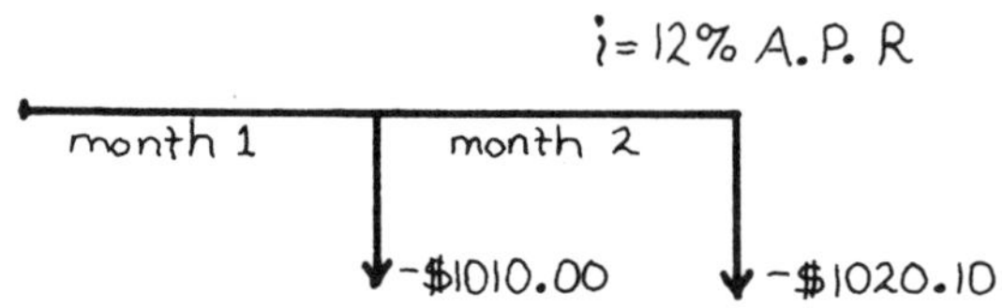

(Hint: 12% is 1% per month; 10 is 1% of 1000; and 10.1 is 1% of 1010.)

2. What is the Net present value of this cash–flow situation?

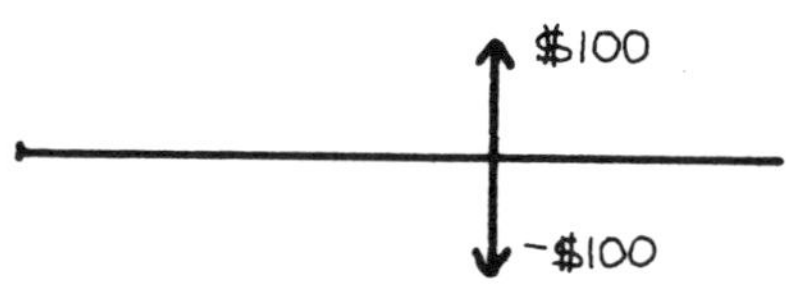

3. What is the Net present value of this cash–flow situation?

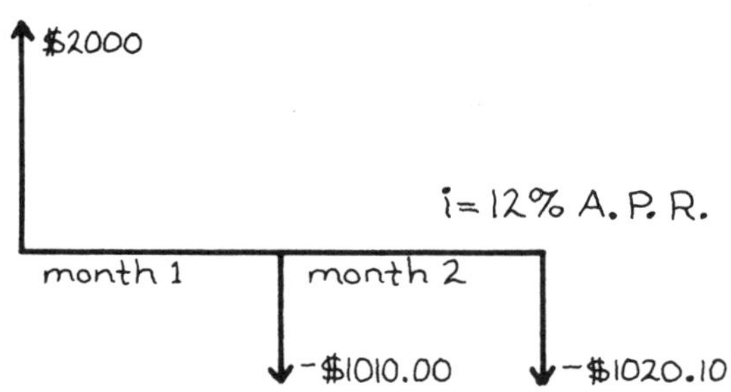

ANSWERS

1. The Net Present Value is –$2000.
   Slide each cash–flow back to the beginning of the time line. First "slide:"

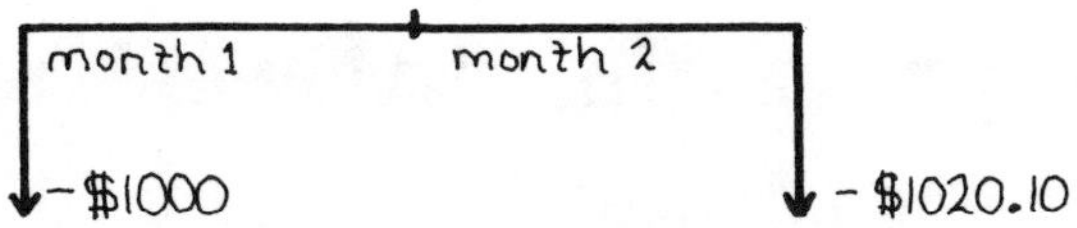

Second "slide:"

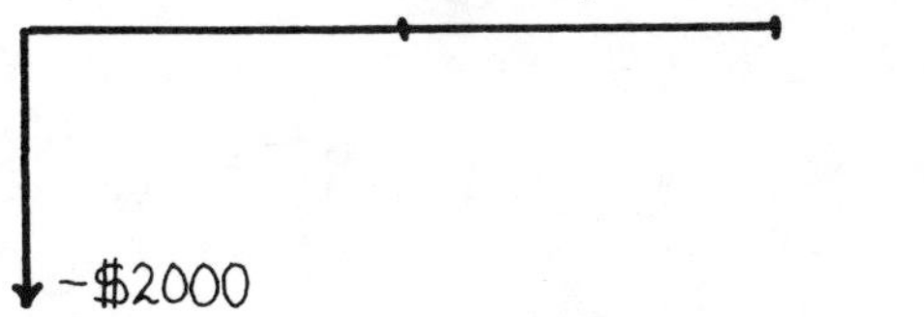

2. Zero. Why? Well, no matter what values these cash–flows take––after being slid back––they will still be equal and opposite and therefore "net" out to be zero, right?

3. Zero.
   This:

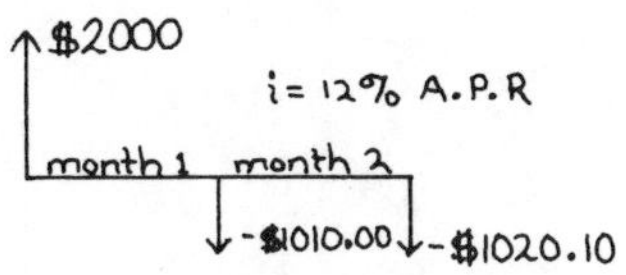

is equivalent to this (look at problem 1):

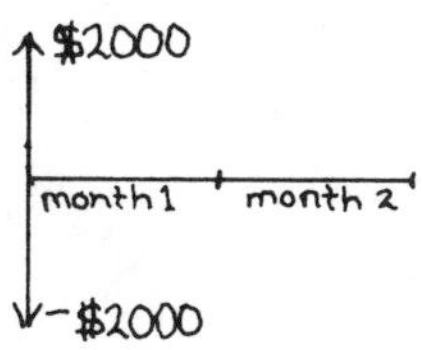

which is zero (look at problem 2).

So, that's what Net Present Value is all about.
If you have a set of uneven cash–flows like this:

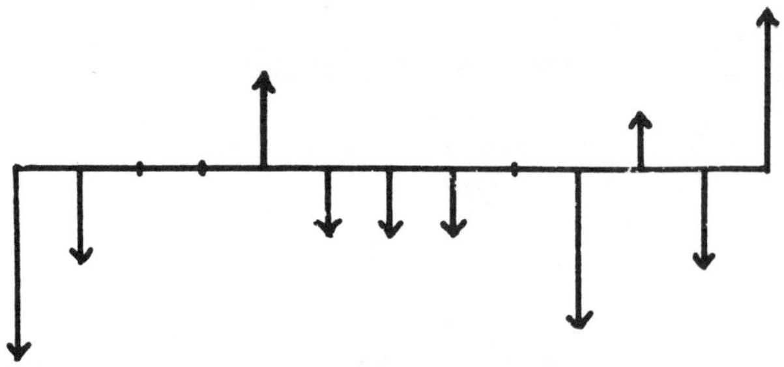

and you know the prevailing interest rate, you can slide all those arrows to the left end of the picture frame and add them together to find a Net Present Value (NPV). And with the [NPV] key it will take just one step to solve this, once the calculator "sees" the cash–flow diagram.

But how do you describe such a picture to the HP–12C?

PAINTING THE PICTURE

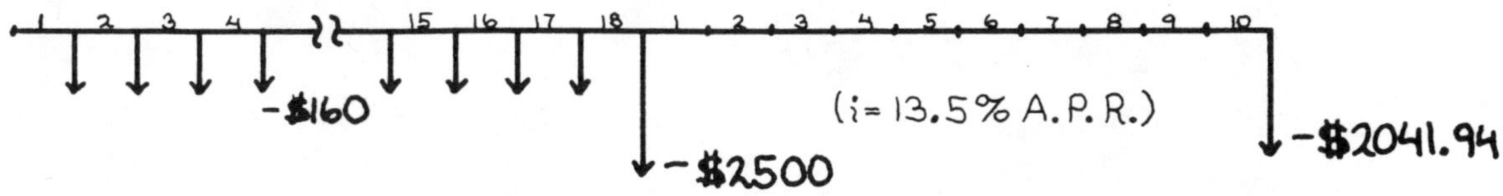

This picture would be easy to describe to one of your friends, but usually it would take about a thousand words.

Now, on the HP–12C, you have just three keys to describe that same picture. With such a limited "vocabulary," it's important that you clearly understand what these three "words" mean to the HP–12C. The three keys are:

[CFo], [CFj], and [Nj].

They're in the top row printed in blue....

With these three keys, you need only relate two facts to the HP–12C. These are:

1. The dollar amount of each cash–flow in a "cash–flow group."

2. The number of cash–flows in a "cash–flow group."

"So what's a cash–flow group?"

Simple, a cash–flow group is a sequence of regular, even, cash–flows. A cash–flow group can consist of only one cash–flow, or it can consist of many.

Here are several cash–flow groups:

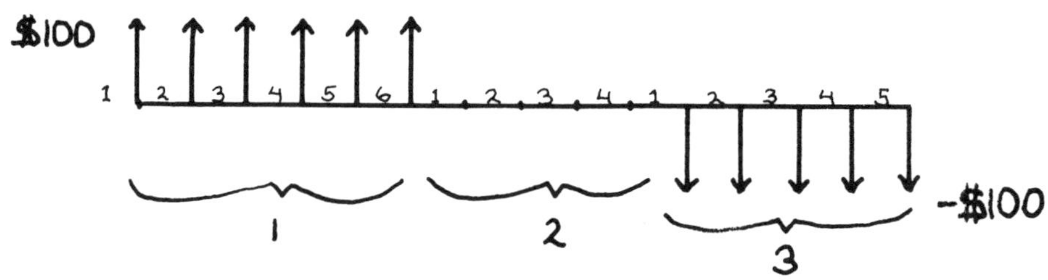

You have to describe these groups in their sequential order, from left to right (present to future).

To describe the first group, you need only mention these two things:

1. The dollar amount of each cash–flow is $100.00.
2. The number of cash–flows in this group is 6.

Look at the second cash–flow group:

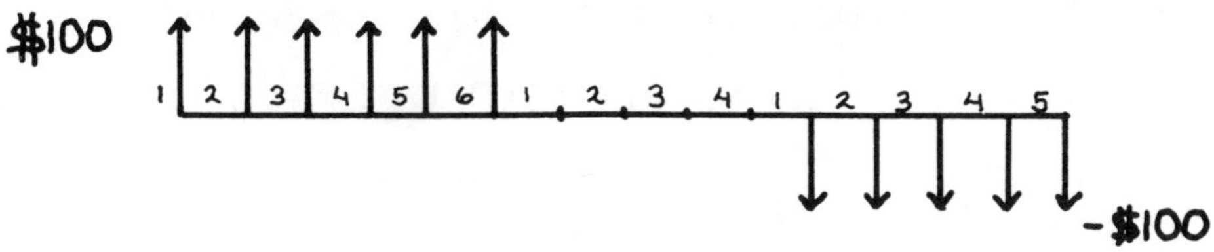

You would say:
1. The dollar amount of each cash–flow is ZERO.
2. The number of cash–flows is 4.

As you can see, when describing an uneven cash–flow situation to the HP–12C, you must describe every period on the cash–flow line. Some periods will have positive cash–flows, some will have negative cash–flows, and some will have cash–flows that equal ZERO. And REMEMBER! ZERO is still a number. You need to be able to think of a period having no cash–flow as a period having a cash–flow with a dollar amount of ZERO.

Finally, look at the last group on that diagram:
1. The dollar amount of each cash–flow is –$100.00.
2. The number of cash–flows in this group is 5.

Pretty easy to describe, is it not? Notice how every period on the diagram is accounted for.

Try this: Describe this uneven cash–flow situation in exactly the same fashion as on the previous page.

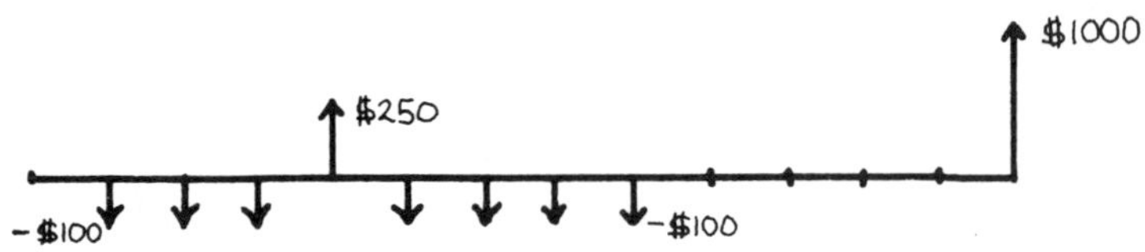

Solution: There are six cash–flow groups on the above diagram. Here's a description.

A. The cash–flow group at the beginning of the time line:

   1. has a dollar amount of $0.
   2. consists of one cash–flow.

B. The next cash–flow group:

   1. has a dollar amount of –$100.
   2. consists of 3 cash–flows.

C. The next cash–flow group:

   1. has a dollar amount of $250.
   2. consists of 1 cash–flow.

D. The next cash–flow group:

1. has a dollar amount of –$100.
2. consists of 4 cash–flows.

E. The next cash–flow group:

1. has a dollar amount of $0.
2. consists of 4 cash–flows.

F. The next cash–flow group:

1. has a dollar amount of $1000.
2. consists of 1 cash–flow.

Do you see what's happening?

You can describe any cash–flow GROUP using only these two phrases:

1. The dollar amount of this cash–flow group is $XXX.XX.

2. This cash–flow group consists of XX cash–flow(s).

Now it's a simple matter to switch to the "language" of the HP–12C.

First, you'll use the [CFo] and [Nj] keys to describe the cash–flow group at the BEGINNING of the time line on a cash–flow diagram. After that, you'll use the [CFj] and [Nj] keys to describe each succeeding cash–flow group. Watch...

Here's the picture of the payment schedule in problem 4 (page 136):

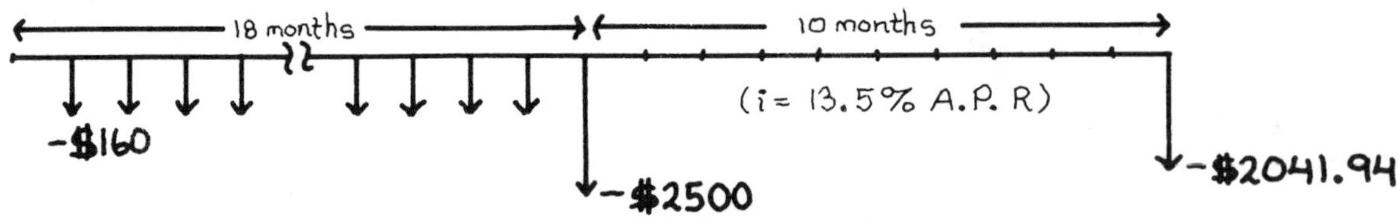

And this is what you have to tell the HP–12C:

CF(0) = 0 — The dollar amount of this (first) cash–flow group is $0.00.

n(0) = 1 — This group consists of 1 cash–flow.

CF(1) = –160 — The dollar amount of this cash–flow group is –$160.00.

n(1) = 17 — This group consists of 17 cash–flows.

CF(2) = –2500 — The dollar amount of this cash–flow group is –$2500.00.

n(2) = 1 — This group consists of 1 cash–flow.

CF(3) = 0
n(3) = 9 — Every period must be accounted for in the picture that you're drawing for the calculator.

CF(4) = –2041.94
n(4) = 1 — Get the idea?

Here's how you key this in:

0 [g] [CFo]
1 [g] [Nj]

The [CFo] key tells the calculator that you're starting to describe a new cash–flow diagram. That's why you use it ONLY for the first cash–flow group.

160 [CHS] [g] [CFj]
17 [g] [Nj]
2500 [CHS] [g] [CFj]

0 [g] [CFj]
9 [g] [Nj]

Notice, for groups consisting of just one cash–flow, you don't have to press 1 [g] [Nj]. You CAN; The HP–12C understands either

2041.94 [CHS] [g] [CFj]

Now that you've described the picture for your calculator, you want to find the Net Present Value (NPV), so just key in the prevailing interest rate:

13.5 [ENTER]
12 [÷] [i]

Now press [f] [NPV]. The answer is –6,000. Hallelujah! This proves the lender's claim (from problem 4 on page 136) to be correct!

POP QUIZ

1. Find the Net Present Value of this cash–flow diagram. The prevailing interest rate is 18.7% (A.P.R.).

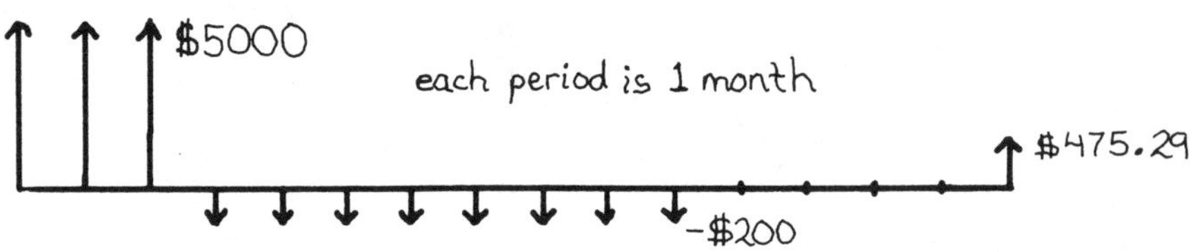

POP ANSWER

1. The answer is $13,700. Here are the keystrokes:

18.7 [ENTER] [12] [÷] [i]

5000 [g] [CFo] 3 [g] [Nj]

200 [CHS] [g] [CFj]
8 [g] [Nj]

0 [g] [CFj]
4 [g] [Nj]

475.29 [g] [CFj]
[f] [NPV]

Now you know what NPV means, and you know how to describe an uneven cash–flow situation to your HP–12C, using the CFo, CFj, and Nj operations.

Next, take a look at NPV's sister operation: IRR.

INTERNAL RATE OF RETURN

When you have a clear understanding of NPV, then IRR (Internal Rate of Return) follows close behind.

There was a problem back on page 151 that looked like this:

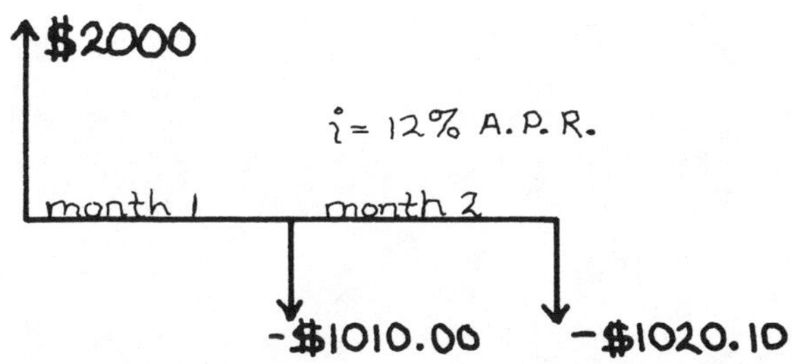

This picture would describe a loan taken out at 12% A.P.R. and paid back in 2 months (but not with level payments, right?).

You were asked to find the NPV of this cash–flow situation. At that time, you were asked to calculate the NPV of this situation without your calculator and you found that the NPV was ZERO.

Now, since you know how to solve for NPV on your calculator, plug in this picture and see if you get an NPV of 0.

2000 [g] [CFo]

1010 [CHS] [g] [CFj]

1020.10 [CHS] [g] [CFj]

Don't forget the interest rate
1 [i]
Now, press [f] [NPV].
Sure enough...it's ZERO!

Try this: Change the interest rate to 15% A.P.R., and recalculate NPV. Will it still be ZERO?

Solution: 15 [ENTER] 12 [÷] [i] [f] [NPV]. The result is NOT zero. The NPV for this picture,

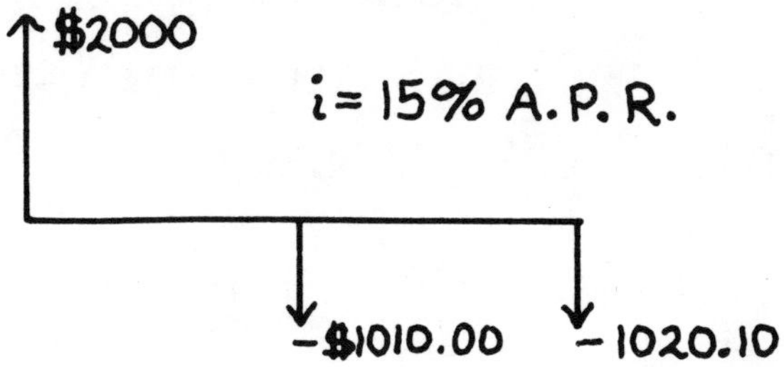

is NOT zero. In fact, there is only one interest rate here that will make the NPV equal to zero.

Now, just for kicks, press [f] [IRR]

Answer: 1

[IRR] is the periodic interest rate that gives this picture an NPV of ZERO.

If you take the complete cash–flow diagram of any completely amortized loan (with even or uneven cash–flows), it will have an NPV of ZERO and the IRR is simply the interest rate of the loan.

Try this: You loan out $1500 and you set up the deal so that this cash–flow diagram completely amortizes the loan in 4 months:

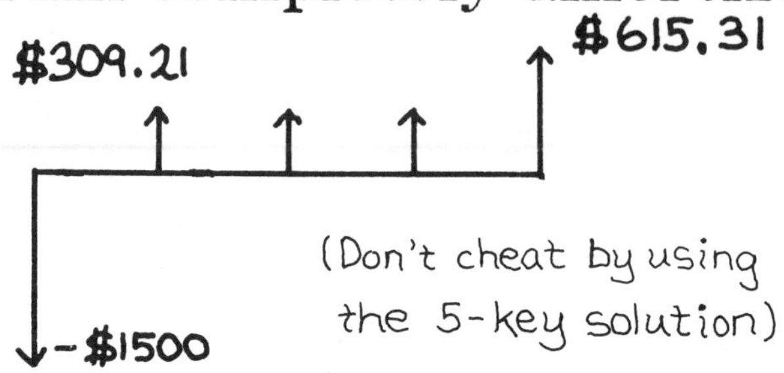

What is the prevailing (A.P.R.) that applies to this cash–flow diagram? In other words, what is the (annualized) IRR of this cash–flow situation?

Solution: 12.2% A.P.R. Here are the keystrokes:

1500 [CHS] [g] [CFo]

309.21 [g] [CFj]
3 [g] [Nj]

615.31 [g] [CFj]

[f] [IRR] (it takes a while)
12 [X]

Do you understand what you're doing when you press [IRR]? Make sure with this short quiz.

POP QUIZ

1. What's the IRR of this cash-flow situation?

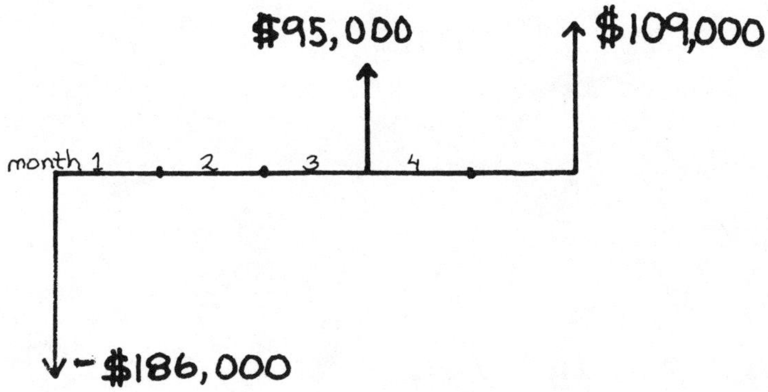

POP ANSWER

1. 27.63% A.P.R.
   Here are the keystrokes:

   186000 [CHS] [g] [CFo]
   0 [g] [CFj] 2 [g] [Nj]
   95000 [g] [CFj]
   0 [g] [CFj]
   109000 [g] [CFj]

   [f] [IRR]
   12 [X]

Again, the only time you have to use the Nj key is when there's more than one cash-flow in a group.

MORE ABOUT KEYING IN UNEVEN CASH–FLOWS

Up to now you may or may not recognize the utility of the two functions NPV and IRR. If you don't, it's no surprise. So far, the quizzes have just blurted out cash–flow diagrams, asking you to compute the NPV's and IRR's.

In an upcoming quiz, you will be faced with several examples that will demonstrate the true usefulness of these functions in investment analysis, but first take another look at the insides of your calculator.

Recall the payment schedule of that loan problem (number 4) from page 136:

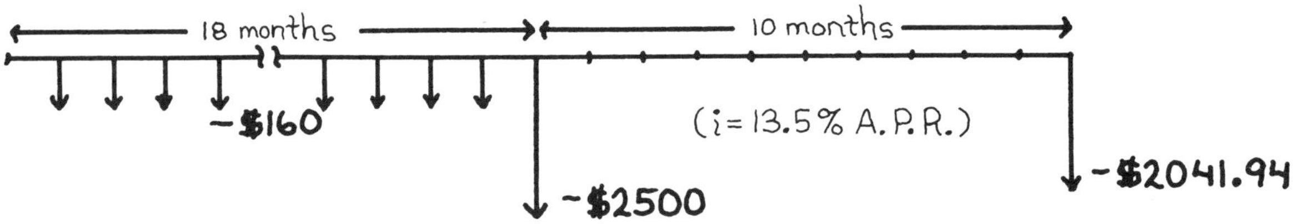

You keyed in this uneven cash–flow situation back on page 160 to find that it had an NPV of –\$6000 to confirm that the lender was telling the truth, as usual.

Now, watch what happens in the storage registers when you go through the keystrokes.

0 [g] [CFo]

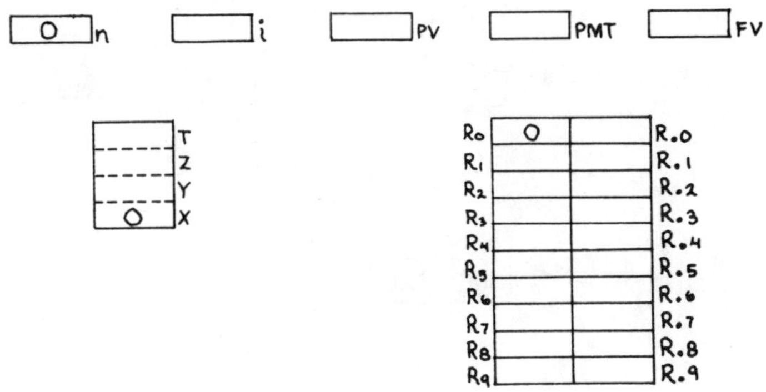

160 [CHS] [g] [CFj]

17 [g] [Nj]

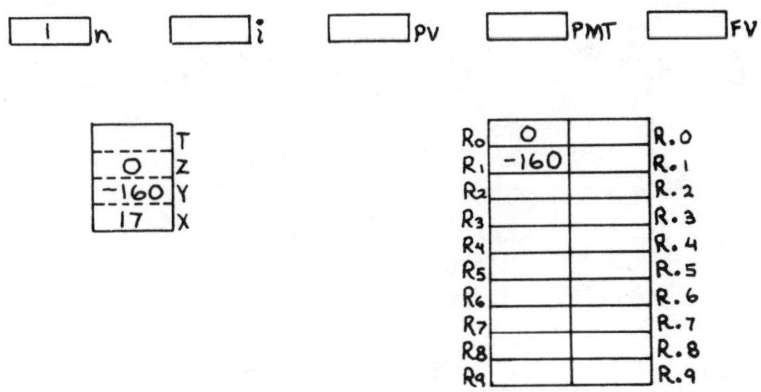

2500 [CHS] [g] [CFj]

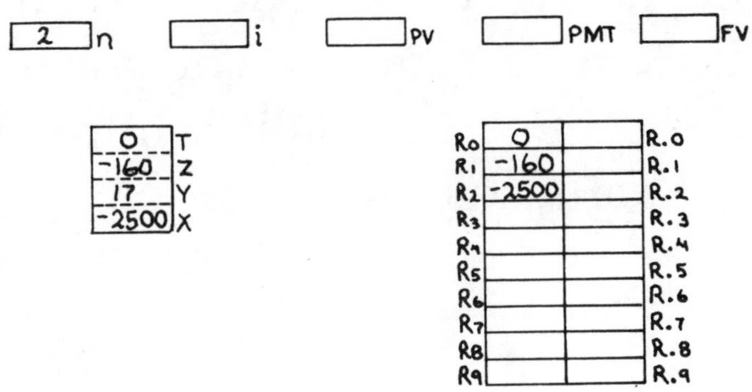

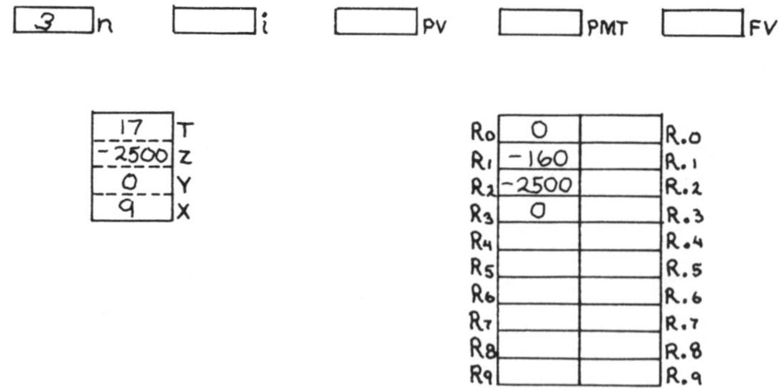

0 g CFj
9 g Nj

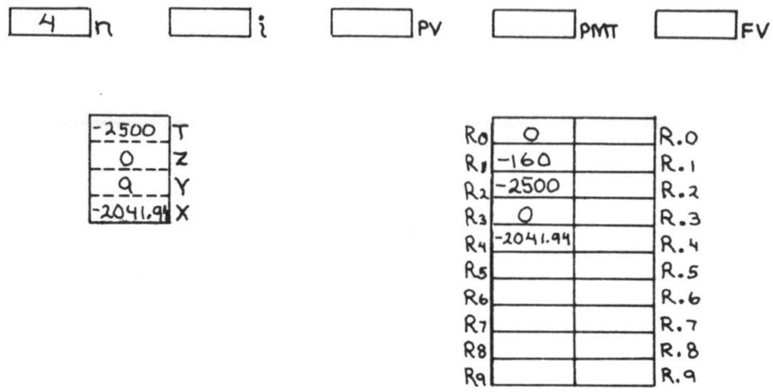

2041.94 CHS g CFj

It's like clockwork, really.

See how the amount of each cash–flow group is stored in the corresponding register? CF(3) in register 3; CF(0) in register 0, etc.

And notice the n–register. It keeps count of the number of groups. The number in the n–register is called "j." And this is where the names "CFj" and "Nj" come from.

When you press [CFo], you start this "j–count" over again at zero. And every time after that, when you press [CFj], that "j" in the n–register is incremented by one. So "j" is the counter––to help the HP–12C piece together the picture you're drawing for it.

But what about the Nj's? Where does the calculator "remember" in this problem, for example, that CFo occurs once, but that CF_1 occurs 17 times?

Well, there are actually 20 "hidden" registers called n_0, n_1, n_2, ..., n_{19}. The Nj's are stored there.

These registers are somewhat "special," not only because they're hidden, but because they can store only whole numbers from 0 to 99. In fact, if you try to store any other number (e.g. if you press 2.3 [g] [Nj] or 100 [g] [Nj]), you'll get a message: ERROR 6.

So how DO you use these registers? Well, you use the "j" value (in the n–register) to "point" to whichever hidden register you want. For example, if the value (i.e. the "j" value) is 2, then [g] [Nj] will copy the contents of the X–register into the "hidden" n_2 register.

Similarly, if the "j" value in the n–register is 5, then [RCL] [g] [Nj] will recall n_5. Work with this a bit until you're comfortable with the idea.

DETAILS OF NPV AND IRR

It's quite easy to think of [NPV] and [IRR] for "uneven cash–flow situations" as being analogous to [PV] and [i] for "even cash–flow" situations.

After all, when you press [NPV], the result is put into the PV register (as well as the X–register); and when you press [IRR], the result is put into the i–register (as well as the X–register). So the analogy is definitely there, but there are important differences that you must know....

It's true that both [PV] and [NPV] are doing the same thing: they're sliding back future cash–flows to the beginning of the time line and adding up the resulting total there. But [PV] "flips" the arrows over (i.e. it changes the signs of the cash–flows) when it does this sliding.

This is because PV and FV are always considered to be opposite ends of a "loan–money–out–get–money–back/ borrow–money–pay–money–back" type of cash–flow situation. By contrast, [NPV] makes no assumptions about what a cash–flow means. It just slides cash–flows back to the beginning of the time line.

You can demonstrate this difference: Solve for the front–end of the same EVEN cash–flow situation twice, once using PV and once using NPV, and you will get the same number from both methods, but they will be of opposite sign. So don't get confused by this; just remember the different assumption each operation is making.

Also, be careful of the analogy between i and IRR.

Don't always try to interpret IRR as the interest rate (i.e. as the "yield" on the money invested), because that's not always the case.

IRR is not ALWAYS the "yield."

For example, it turns out mathematically that in some cash–flow situations, there can be more than one IRR! There can be more than one interest rate that will produce an NPV of zero! And in other situations, there might be no IRR at all! (This is discussed more in Appendix V.)

So when things like this happen––and they do––don't even TRY to envision IRR as your "yield." All bets are off.

Now test your understanding of [NPV] and [IRR] with these problems....

TEST--NPV AND IRR

(answers will follow)

Remember to draw those cash–flow diagrams!

1. A loan is written at 15% A.P.R., with $450 monthly payments, in arrears, for 30 years. What is the loan amount? Find it by using the NPV operation on your calculator. (No cheating with the 5–keys!) Do the same for annuity in advance.

(If you get an ERROR message here, don't hesitate to look at the solution.)

2. As an investor, you're offered a chance to "buy" a double mortgage from a lender.

   The first mortgage was written for $90,000 for 30 years, with end–of–the–month payments at 12% A.P.R. After 15 years a second mortgage for $30,000 was added, at 13.0% for 20 years, with monthly payments also in arrears.

   If you want to obtain a 16% yield (A.P.R.) on the money you invest, what should you pay for the right to "inherit" this contract at the end of the third year of the second mortgage?

(You have all the knowledge you need to do this one. Take your time and work it through; then look at the solution.)

3. On that double mortgage from the previous problem, well, it turns out that you managed to chew the price down to $75,000. What was your resulting yield?

4. How much money should you deposit in a bank account that pays 8% A.P.R., compounded monthly, so that you can withdraw $10,000 per quarter for 20 years, starting 20 years from now? What about $15,000 withdrawals?

5. How much will you have accumulated in a bank account paying 6% compounded daily, if you follow this weekly deposit schedule?

YEAR	WEEKLY DEPOSIT
1	$5
2	$10
3	$15
4	$20
5	$25
6	$30
7	$35
8	$40
9	$45
10	$50

6. You have $20,000 and you're moving to a new town for a 5–year contract job. A quick check of that town's housing market shows that you can buy a $95,000 home for the $20,000 down, $400 monthly (interest only) payments in arrears, and about $200 a month in taxes, insurance, and maintenance. And after the 5 years, with the way things are going, you can expect to sell it for $120,000.

   On the other hand, you can rent that same house for $600 per month (paid at the beginning of the month) and just salt away your $20,000 in a money market at 12% A.P.R. (compounded monthly).

   Given these scenarios, should you rent or buy? ("To buy or not to buy--that is the question.")

TEST SOLUTIONS

1. Here's the picture you have to draw for your calculator:

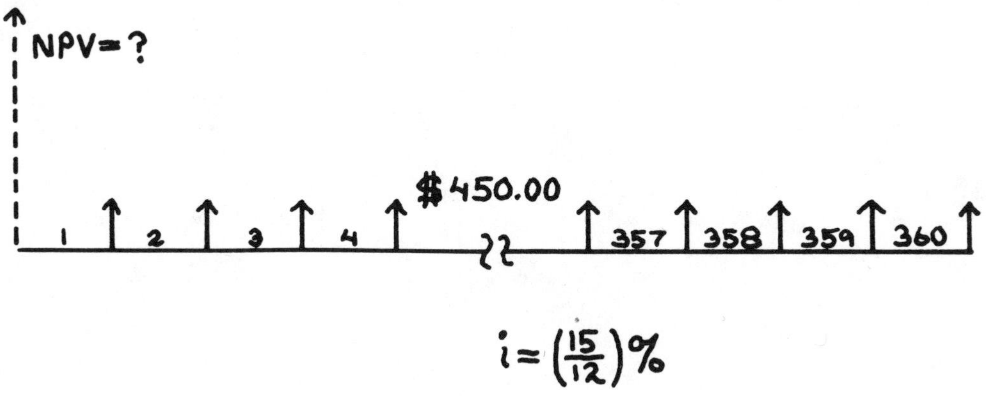

You need to use NPV to find that dotted–arrow amount the "purchase amount" of the loan.

Nothing to it:

0 [g] [CFo]	(No cash–flow occurs at the beginning.)
450 [g] [CFj]	
360 [g] [Nj]	

Whoops! What's wrong?

Remember from page 170, the greatest number that will fit in an Nj register is 99.

To get around this, just put in 4 consecutive groups of 90 cash–flows, each $450.

(First, just press any key to clear the ERROR message.)

90 [g] [Nj]

450 [g] [CFj]
[X<>Y] [g] [Nj]

[X<>Y] [g] [CFj]

Since the 450 and the 90 are already in the stack, why bother keying them repeatedly?

[X<>Y] [g] [Nj]

[X<>Y] [g] [CFj]
[X<>Y] [g] [Nj]

(Pretty easy, isn't this?)

Now put in the prevailing interest rate:

15 [ENTER] 12 [÷] [i]

and solve for NPV: [f] [NPV] Answer: 35,588.76

That was the loan amount for annuity in arrears.

What about for annuity in advance? Can you just switch to BEGIN mode?

NO!

The [BEG] and [END] keys don't work for NPV. You have to draw the picture explicitly:

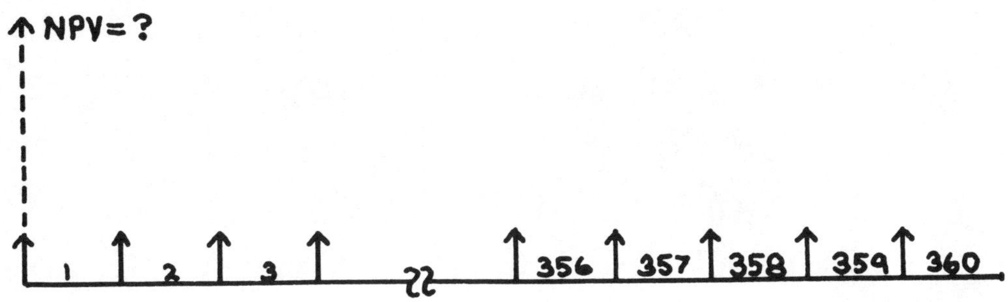

But don't start all over! After all, there are only two changes you need to make.

1. CF(0) = 450, instead of zero.
2. There are 359 other cash–flows, instead of 360.

Don't use [g] [CFo], or else you'll reset the n–register back to zero. Just press 450 [STO] 0. (If this confuses you, review pages 154 to 161, and take your time.)

The n–register still has 4 in it (test this: RCL [n]) signifying 4 cash–flow groups. But now there's only 89 in the fourth group, not 90. Since there's still a 4 in the n–register, all you have to press is: 89 [g] [Nj]. That makes n(4) equal to 89.

Finally, press [f] [NPV]. Answer: 36,033.62

2. This is a simple problem when you draw the picture.

As the investor, you take the perspective of the lender. You pay out a certain amount at the beginning of the time line and you will receive payments according to the specified schedule. Of course, you want those payments to amount to an overall yield of 16% A.P.R. on the money you paid out. You can find the proper amount to pay out by computing the Net Present Value of all those future cash–flows. This NPV will be positive, meaning that you will be receiving the equivalent of that much money when you "buy" this cash–flow situation.

Here's the situation at the time you're offered the deal:

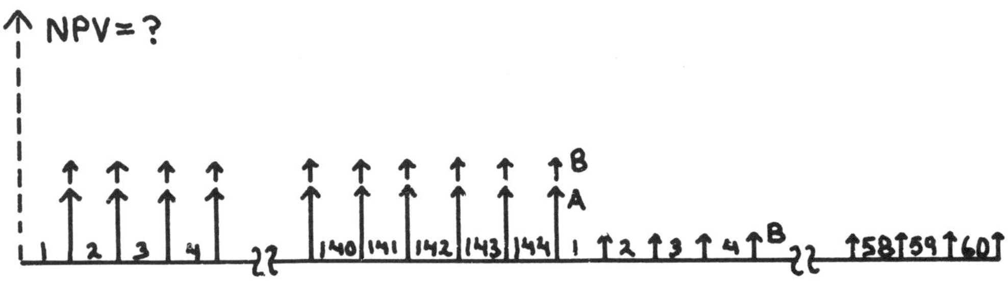

For 12 years you'll receive payments on both the first and second mortgages (144 combined payments). After those 12 years, payments on the first mortgage will stop, but payments on the second mortgage will continue for 5 more years (60 payments). It's all there on the picture.

First, you need to find the payment amounts on each mortgage:

A. The payment on the first mortgage.

90,000 [CHS] [PV]
360 [n]
1 [i] (12% compounded monthly)
0 [FV] (completely amortized)

[PMT] Answer: 925.75

(Pshaw! That was easy!)

Now, don't write anything down or store anything in a register. This whole problem can be done using just the stack.

B. The payment on the second mortgage.

30,000 [CHS] [PV]
240 [n]
13 [ENTER] 12 [÷] [i]
0 [FV] [PMT] Answer: 351.47

Now add the two payments (press [+]).

Answer: 1,277.22

That is the amount of the first 144 payments. The last 60 payments will just be the amount of the payment for the second mortgage. "OH NO! Where is that amount saved? It was just added to the amount of the first mortgage payment! It's gone!"

Don't worry. It's still in the PMT–register.

Now you're ready to draw the picture for the calculator:

0 [g] [Cfo]
[R↓] [g] [CFj]
99 [g] [Nj]
[R↓] [g] [CFj]
45 [g] [Nj]
[RCL] [PMT] [g] [CFj]
60 [g] [Nj]

(Remember the trick for groups larger than 99?)

You want to obtain a yield of 16% A.P.R. on your investment. So press 16 [ENTER] 12 [÷] [i].

Finally, pressing [f] [NPV] will tell the HP–12C to calculate the amount you should pay for the right to "inherit" this cash–flow scenario so that your money will earn 16% A.P.R. That amount is $83,714.73.

3. Here's the situation (This is an easy one):

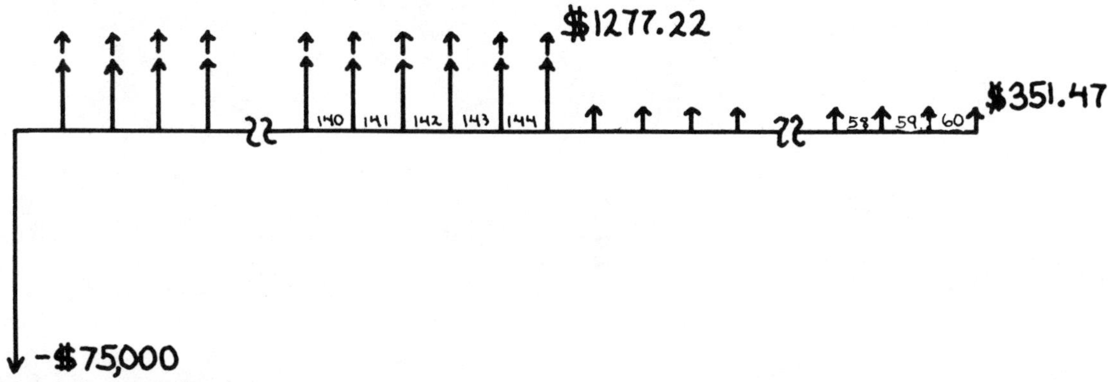

Just draw the picture...

75,000 [CHS] [g] [CFo] (Don't forget that this has to be negative--you're paying it.)

1277.22 [g] [CFj] 99 [g] [Nj]
[R↓] [g] [CFj] 45 [g] [Nj]
351.47 [g] [CFj] 60 [g] [Nj]
...and turn the crank (it takes a while).
[f] [IRR] Answer: 1.5472

(Gulp!) That's a whole lot smaller than the yield in the original problem. What gives? Shouldn't it be a bigger yield?

Hold your horses. This is a monthly IRR. It still has to be annualized (multiplied by 12). Right?

12 [X] Answer: 18.57

That's better.

4. Here's the situation:

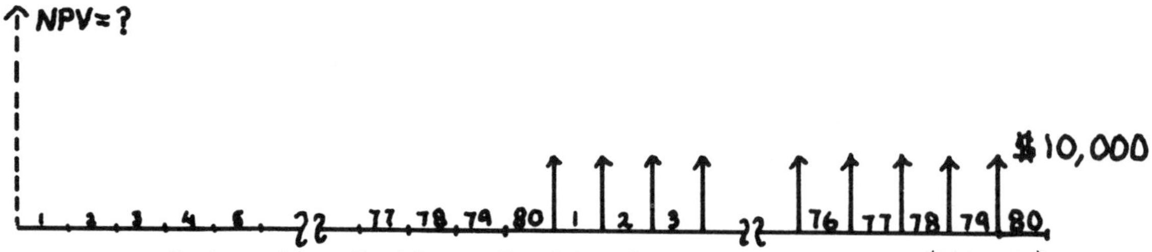

Again, you need to find the dotted up–arrow (NPV).

This is easy, as long as you convert to the proper interest rate:

12 [n]
8 [ENTER] 12 [÷] [i]
100 [CHS] [PV]
0 [PMT] [FV] Answer: 108.30

4 [n] [i] Answer: 2.0134

That's the quarterly rate that accrues the same amount on $100 in a year as does 8/12% monthly. And it's now in the i–register, so leave it there.

The rest is easy:

0 [g] [CFo] 80 [g] [Nj]
10,000 [g] [CFj] 80 [g] [Nj]

[f] [NPV] Answer: 81,967.88

For $15,000 withdrawals, just change CF(1):

15,000 [STO] 1
[f] [NPV] Answer: 122,951.83

5. The problem here is to find a net FUTURE value, isn't it? You're trying to figure out what this whole cash–flow mess is worth at the OTHER end of the time line.

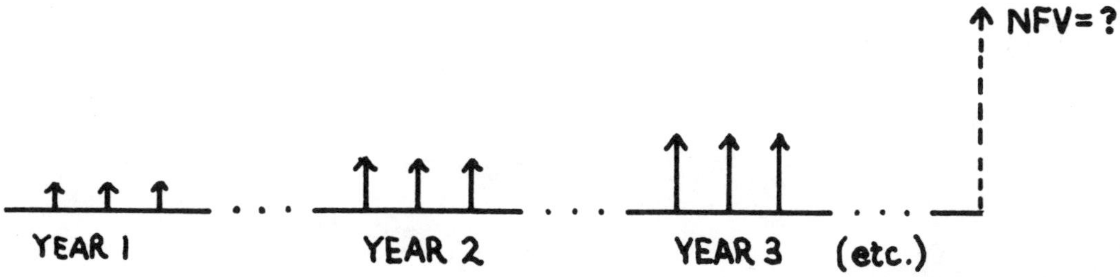

But there's no NFV key, so you have to get creative (surely you've heard of creative financing).

Here's what you do: First, find the NPV. By doing this, you're "sliding" all the cash–flows back to the beginning of the 10 years.

Next, just compute the FV that results from accruing the interest on that one lump sum for 10 years. That "slides" the NPV to the end of the 10 years time line to make it an "NFV."

Of course, you need to convert the bank's daily compounding rate to an equivalent weekly rate to match the intervals of your deposits.

6 [ENTER] 365 [n] [÷] [i] (Assume this bank counts days just like NASA does.)

100 [CHS] [PV]
0 [PMT]
[FV] Answer: 106.18
52 [n] [i] Answer: 0.1154

Again, leave the result in the i-register--you've got it right where you want it.

Now, just draw the picture:

5 [CHS] [g] [CFo] 52 [g] [Nj]
10 [CHS] [g] [CFj] 52 [g] [Nj]
15 [CHS] [g] [CFj] 52 [g] [Nj]
20 [CHS] [g] [CFj] 52 [g] [Nj]
25 [CHS] [g] [CFj] 52 [g] [Nj]
30 [CHS] [g] [CFj] 52 [g] [Nj]
35 [CHS] [g] [CFj] 52 [g] [Nj]
40 [CHS] [g] [CFj] 52 [g] [Nj]
45 [CHS] [g] [CFj] 52 [g] [Nj]
50 [CHS] [g] [CFj] 52 [g] [Nj]

Then press: [f] [NPV] Answer: –9,797.28

All those deposits are worth 9,797.28 if you slide them to the beginning of the time line.

Now, just let this accrue for 10 years. After all, you slid all those cash–flows back to the beginning, and you can jolly well move them forward to the other end of the line, as long as you let the prevailing interest rate increase the amount accordingly.

NOTICE THAT the NPV operation always leaves its result in the PV–register as well as the X–register (that's handy). Leave it there!

520 [n]	(520 weeks in 10 years, right?)
0 [PMT]	(Just sliding––no payments.)
[FV]	Answer: 17,850.93

6. Here are the two situations, side by side, for comparison.

(Do these look like the diagrams you drew?)

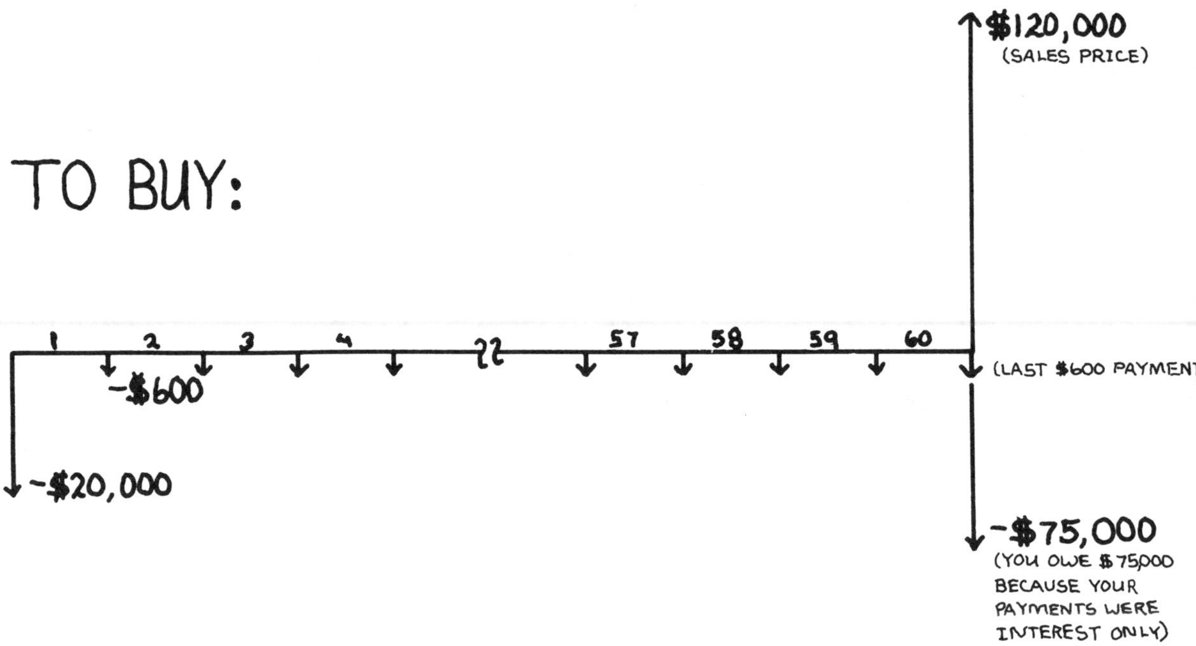

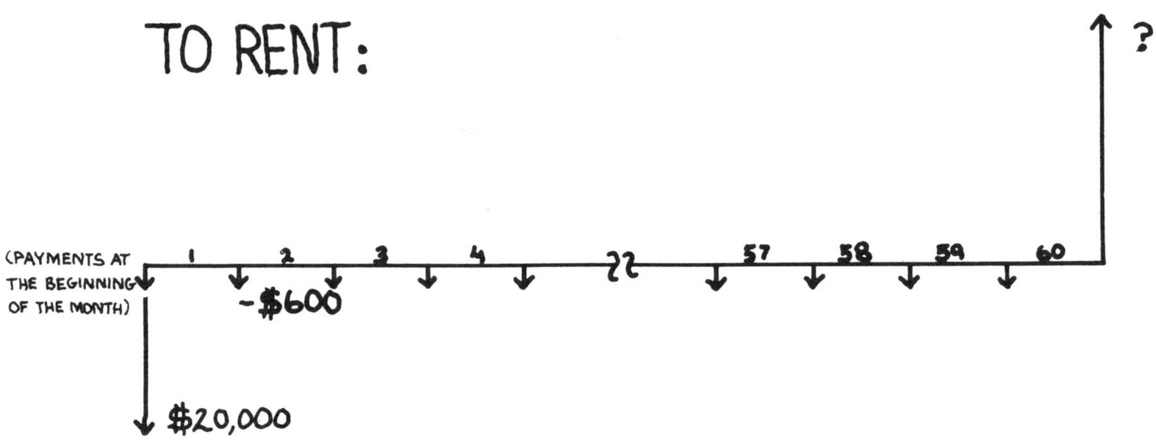

The first thing to do is to figure out the final cash–flow in the "rent" picture.

How much will $20,000 grow into in 5 years of accrual at 12% A.P.R. compounded monthly?

By now this solution ought to be a piece of cake (or easy as pie.)

20,000 [CHS] [PV]
60 [n]
1 [i]
0 [PMT]
[FV] Answer: 36,333.93
(A nice little nest egg.)

Now the pictures are complete. So, to compare them, just draw each picture for your calculator, and ask for the IRR. The higher "yield" (or the lower cost to you) is the better choice.

Draw the "rent" picture.

20,600 [CHS] [g] [CFo] (Payments at the beginning of the month.)

600 [CHS] [g] [CFj] 59 [g] [Nj]
[RCL] [FV] [g] [CFj]
[f] [IRR] 12 [X] Answer: –13.32

Now draw the "buy" picture:

20,000 [CHS] [g] [CFo]
600 [CHS] [g] [CFj] 59 [g] [Nj]
120,000 [ENTER] 75,600 [–] [g] [CFj]
(Payments at the end of the month.)
[f] [IRR] 12 [X] Answer: –6.67

Because of the fact that both pictures show a negative yield, you aren't making money either way. However, you'll be minimizing your "living costs" by BUYING the house.

The key to this problem is in realizing that your $20,000 is going to be an investment in either case, and all you need to do is to compare the yields.

But what would you have done if one or both of these scenarios turned out to have multiple IRR's––or no IRR at all?

Well, you can still compare investments by using NPV (you can always find exactly one NPV). Keep in mind that the going "price" of money is 12% (i.e. 1% per month), so that's your discount rate.

Since you have all the numbers keyed in for the "buy" picture, just key in: 1 [i] [f] [NPV].

Answer: –22,202.79

So, BUYING the house, and making all those monthly payments is equivalent to shelling out $22,202.79 right when you move in, assuming that the cost of money is 12% A.P.R.

Now look at the "rent" picture.

20,600 [CHS] [g] [CFo]
600 [CHS] [g] [CFj] 59 [g] [Nj]
36,333.93 [g] [CFj]

1 [i] [f] [NPV]   Answer: –27,242.76

RENTING the house, making monthly rental payments, and keeping your $20,000 in the money market is equivalent to shelling out $27,242.76 right when you move in, assuming that the cost of money is 12% A.P.R.

Buying is the better deal (as long as you're reasonably sure about that selling price and the cost of money).

At this point in the Easy Course in Using the HP–12C, you've acquired most of the skills you need to tackle any problems that arise.

And now there's only one other major aspect of the HP–12C that you need to look at.

On this subject, the HP–12C stands alone––separate from all other financial calculators, so it's critical to understand....

Non–Integer n.

(...much wailing and gnashing of teeth...)

Throughout this book, not a word has yet been said about solving for n. It's always been one of the KNOWN quantities.

Look back (just once more) at that loan problem (number 4, page 136).

Suppose that loan had gotten paid off smoothly--just 49 straight monthly installments of $160. The remaining balance at the end would have been 0, right?

Try it:

[g] [END]
49 [n]
13.5 [ENTER] 12 [÷] [i]
6000 [PV]
160 [CHS] [PMT]

Solve for the remaining balance: [FV] Answer: 2.95

"That's positive!" (So was PV.)

"The law has been broken!" (Bar the doors.)

What's happening here? (Read on....)

Well, what's the balance after 48 PMT's?

48 [n] [FV] Answer: –155.31

There's less than $160 remaining after 48 months, and apparently, the interest earned in the 49th month isn't enough to make up the difference.

So how many periods does this loan take to amortize? More than 48 but less than 49, obviously, but how much more or less?

Well, you can't answer that question until you invent the rules.

("Say what??")

You need to decide how interest accrues BETWEEN each end of the D.I.P. In other words, how does interest accrue within the compounding period? You know how much money is owed at the end of the month, but how does that sum grow DURING that month to reach the next "checkpoint?"

(This is one of those subtleties about interest that was mentioned on page 81. It's come back to haunt you....)

There are two common ways that are used to define how interest accrues between the "checkpoints."

A. STRAIGHT–LINE
B. CONTINUOUS COMPOUNDING

Take a close look at these:

A. Straight–line accrual.

This method is fairly easy to understand. The interest earned at any point within the compounding period is proportional to the fraction of the period elapsed. If you're halfway through the period, you've earned half of that period's interest; if you're a third of the way through it, you've earned a third of the interest, etc.

Here's how it looks on paper:

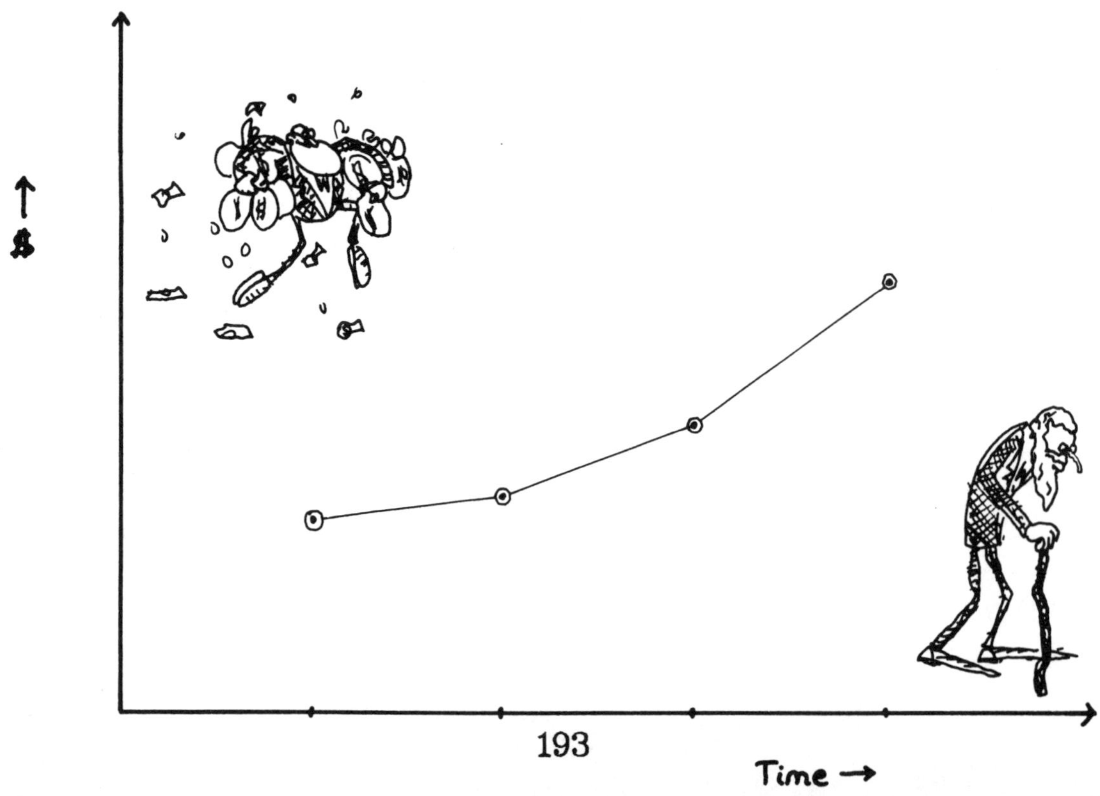

As you can see, the interest goes in straight line segments from "checkpoint" to "checkpoint."

This doesn't mean that interest accrual goes in a straight line overall. You're still looking at compound interest here, and you can see this by looking at the "checkpoints," which are defined by the D.I.R.

Those points still form the old familiar upward–curving compound growth pattern.

B. Continuous Compounding

This method is even easier to picture. The interest accrual within any compounding period behaves exactly the same as the overall curve.

The segments between the "checkpoints" are curved upward--unlike the segments in the STRAIGHT-LINE method.

Here's how these two methods look when put on the same picture:

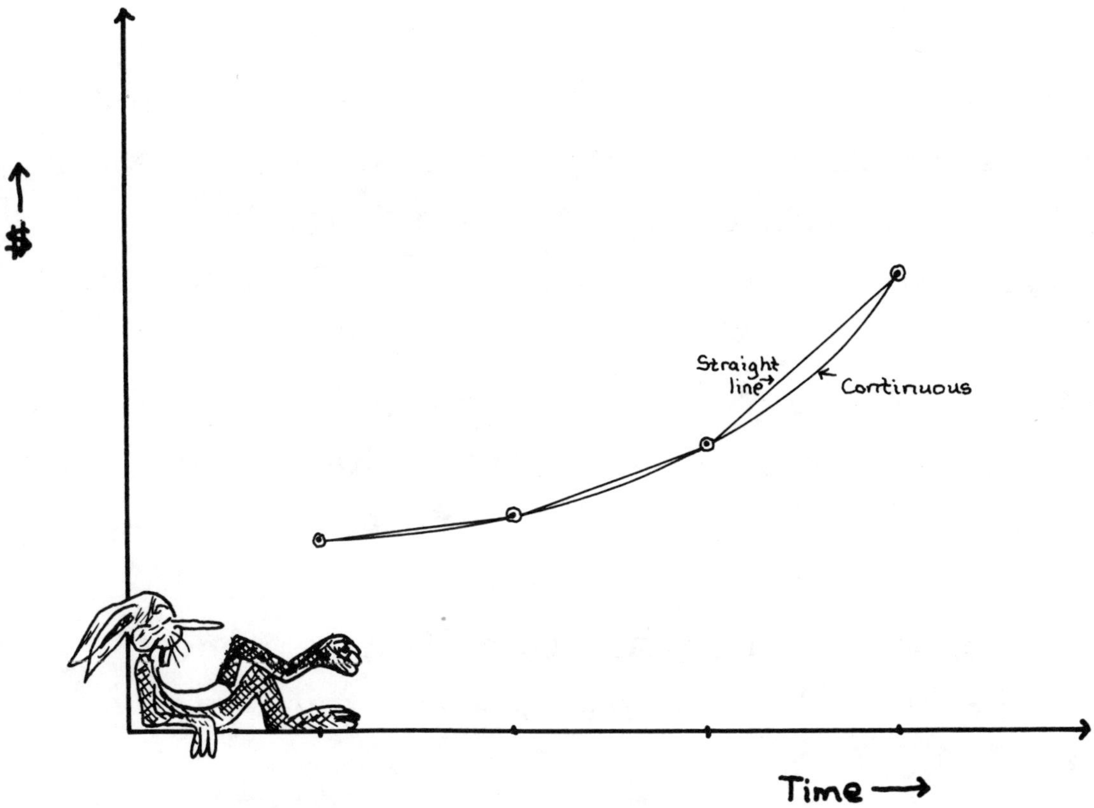

Notice that if you take a snapshot of two comparable bank balances somewhere between the endpoints of the D.I.P. (between the checkpoints), the balance using the straight–line method has more money in it.

Of course, at each checkpoint (once every D.I.P.) the balances are identical, as they must be to have the same D.I.R.

It turns out that with the HP–12C, you can choose which assumption you want the machine to use in working with partial compounding periods (non–integer "n").

If you press [STO] [EEX], you'll see a little "C" appear in the display. That means the method is now CONTINUOUS COMPOUNDING for partial–period accrual.

Press [STO] [EEX] again and the "C" will disappear. Now you've selected straight–line accrual for partial periods.

But REMEMBER! This choice is not a choice between simple and compound interest. Your calculator is still using compound interest to determine the "checkpoints" at each D.I.P., no matter what your choice is. What you're choosing is the path to reach those "checkpoints."

The HP–12C is the first HP financial calculator to offer this choice. The older models use continuous compounding only:

HP–37 HP–38 HP–67/97 (with HP pac software)
HP–41 (with HP module software)

And it's nice to have the choice, because the well–known "Truth–In–Lending" law (also called "Regulation Z") uses the straight–line method.

So, if you're a lender or a borrower, you can correctly quote or confirm an A.P.R. with the HP–12C.

"So THAT'S how you figure out the true n–value in problem 4! Just pick one of these methods and then grind out the answer, right?"

Not so fast! Look what happens when you try that with problem number 4.

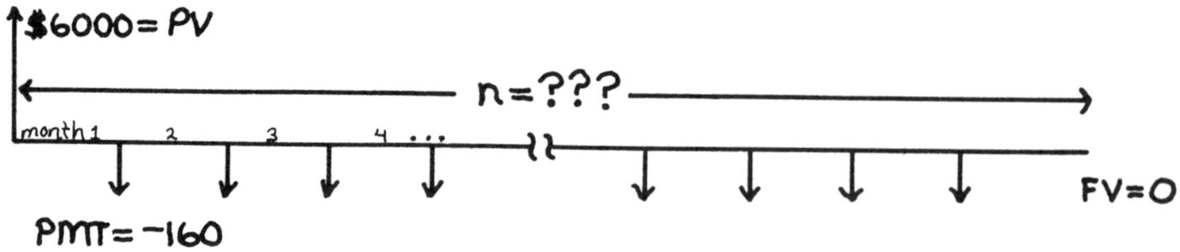

Pick either method. Then:

13.5 [ENTER] 12 [÷] [i]
6000 [CHS] [PV]
160 [PMT]
0 [FV]
[n] Answer: 49.00

"But, that's wrong! 49 payments are too many--I've already proven that. Why is the HP-12C insisting this is the correct answer?"

It's not insisting--that's not the correct answer. It's only an approximation, and it's as close as you're going to get with the HP-12C.

"But why? All the older models give the right answer: 48.9814...!"

No, they don't either. They also give only an approximation--a different one, but still an approximation.

"But that can't be true! There are whole branches of accounting and real estate based upon those older calculations. They HAVE to be right!"

Well, as long as everybody agrees on those calculations (called "actuarial calculations," by the way), you can probably think of them as correct, and there's little harm done.

But they're not numerically correct; they don't actually mean very much, despite the name.

(Actually, the actual meaning of the word "actuarial" is far from the meaning of the word "actual." Actuarial actually implies a statistical nature to these calculations; whereas, the actual, numerically correct results would actually have little to do with actual statistics.)

Hard to believe? Look at the number produced by that solution for [n], using the older calculators:

48.98148...

Now what, pray tell, does this mean?

Does it mean that 98.15% of the way through month 49, you owe $160? No, that can't be right. You don't even owe that much for the whole month.

Does it mean that at 98.15% of the way through month 49, you owe 98.15% of $160 (which comes to $157.04)? No, you'll find that at the END of 49th month, you owe $157.05, and certainly you pay more than a penny of interest in that last day or so (over 3 cents, actually).

That's close, but it's still not right on, and the "closeness" of the approximation will vary with the numbers involved. Want to play dice with the numbers in your bank balance?

The HP–12C AND all the older models give approximate results when you solve for [n] and the answer is not an exact integer. The HP–12C will round up to the next integer. The older models will produce a non–integer value.

"Well, why don't they give correct results?"

Very simply put, the mathematical formula used to compute compound interest with the 5–key solutions applies only when n is an integer. Under any other circumstances, you're trying to make orange juice out of apples; the question, "What is n?", simply has no answer.

Now take the case from the other side: What if you KNOW what n is, but it's non–integer?

Well, the same rule applies: That general 5–key formula is only correct when n IS an integer, and no one–step calculation will produce correct results.

HOWEVER, there are circumstances where the calculators CAN correctly allow for partial periods. They can sometimes cheat––by performing a two–step calculation that looks like one step to you.

For example, on any of the models (HP–12C included), you CAN get correct results with a (known) non–integer n, whenever PMT = 0.

In addition, the HP–12C will give you correct results for non–integer n and NON–zero PMT, IF and ONLY IF the partial period occurs at the BEGINNING of the time line.

So how does this all relate to problem 4? Well, first of all, you should forget all about trying to solve for n; there's simply no better answer than "more than 48 but less than 49."

You can, however, solve for the correct remaining balance at the end of the 49th month, but because that odd period in problem 4 was at the END of the timeline, you can't even get the HP–12C to tell you THAT answer in one calculation.

You have to do the two parts of the calculation yourself....

Here are the two steps you would use to find that remaining balance:

1. Solve for the FV after 49 months (and 49 payments). That positive number means you over-paid the lender in the final month, so the balance is due to YOU as a "rebate," of sorts.

   Answer: 2.95 (You already did this, right?)

2. Just subtract that amount from $160 (the amount of the payment) and you'll find what you really owe as the final 49th installment of the loan.

Answer: 157.05

You Have Been Warned!

When n is the unknown you're solving for, the answer will be correct ONLY when it turns out to be an EXACT integer. On the HP–12C, you can check this by using your resulting n to calculate some other (known) quantity. If that quantity isn't the same as it was before, you know that the whole number given for n was an approximation.

And for when n is KNOWN to be (and input as) a non–integer, here's a summary of what the HP Financial Calculators will do in a single calculation:

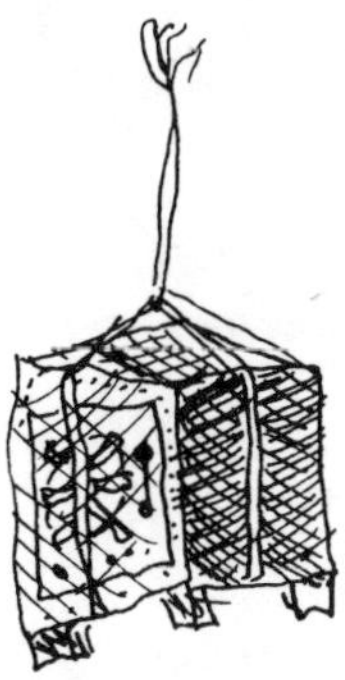

Situation				Will it be handled correctly in one 5-key solution?	
n	PMT	Partial-period accrual method	Location of partial period	HP-12C	HP models 37, 38, 67/97*, 41*
integer	any	either	(no partial period)	YES	YES
non-integer	zero	continuous	either end	YES	YES
non-integer	zero	straight-line	either end	YES	NO
non-integer	non-zero	either	front end	YES	NO
non-integer	non-zero	either	back end	NO	NO

* with HP software or module

Remember that the other calculators will use only continuous compounding during the partial period. But with the HP–12C, you have a choice of continuous compounding or straight–line.

So, that's about it––you've finished the course.

("Yahoo!")

The appendices that follow have many more topics for you to learn about, but they're all optional.

As you can see, there are a lot of considerations involved in financial calculations, but most problems break down into a few easy steps.

Look at what you know:

A. You know how to store and recall numbers, perform arithmetic in the stack, adjust the display and use the prefix keys.

B. You know how to use...
   1. The 5–key solutions (n, i, PV, PMT, FV)
   2. The discounted cash–flow solutions (NPV, IRR)

C. You know how non–integer "n" works and how it doesn't work.

D. You know that if you get half the mileage with that car as we did with that car loan, you'll have made the best buy of your life.

The End

APPENDICES

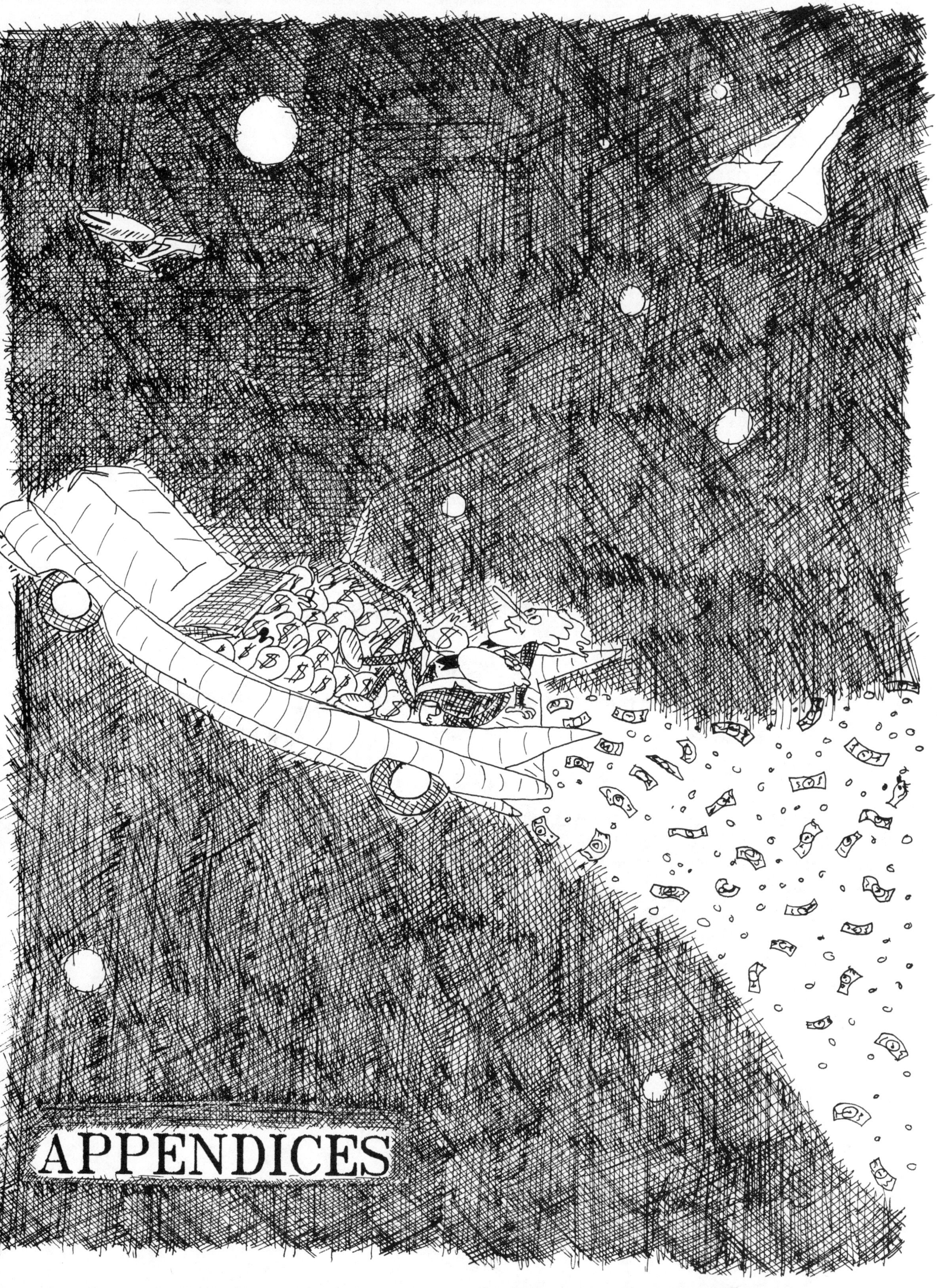

APPENDIX I. On Using The Manual

The HP–12C Owner's Handbook (hereafter called "the manual") you received with your calculator is a thorough and carefully prepared technical manual. It fully documents the workings of your calculator. The more you work with the manual, the more you will appreciate it.

But it's also true that few people really enjoy reading technical manuals. Often, it's not obvious where to begin, or what to learn first. That's one of the reasons for this book. Our aim here was to bring you "up to speed" quickly and memorably, getting you to learn the fundamentals first, then building upon those fundamentals with useful examples.

Of course, we couldn't cover all the details of the manual, and it would be foolish even to try. HP has done a tremendous and meticulous job, and we can add nothing. But we wanted to lay the conceptual groundwork here so that you would be free to use the manual as a reference guide (like a dictionary or encyclopedia), rather than as a tutorial course in financial problem–solving.

We will avoid, as best we can, referring to page numbers in the manual, because we've no guarantee that the manual we're looking at is the same edition that you have.

With that in mind, we should point out some features that can help you refer to it as you need to....

The subject index is the best place to look for answers, assuming you know the proper name of the subject you want. Here are some suggested names:

For anything strange happening in the DISPLAY, try looking under DISPLAY.

For problems with any key, look for that key in its alphabetical order. It will have a box around it.

For a quick check on what an operation does, look in the blue-shaded Function Key Index, just prior to the Subject Index.

For a list of errors and their sources, see Appendix C in the manual.

For a list of the mathematical formulas used by the HP-12C, see Appendix D in the manual.

The other Appendices that follow in THIS book contain some points we thought were important for you to know when you're solving problems with your financial calculator. Your manual contains further information on these subjects, and unless stated otherwise, you can find these subjects in the subject index of the manual.

APPENDIX II.
Depreciation and Statistics

There are some self–explanatory calculations on depreciation––complete with examples (around page 78) in our edition of the manual.

You'll note that the ACRS is not one of the options, and there are two reasons for this:

1. The HP–12C was produced before the advent of ACRS.
2. ACRS cannot be reduced to a simple mathematical formula––tables are required. Parts of the schedule are readily computable, but not all of it. Besides, since tables take up far more memory than it was born with, the HP–12C can't use ACRS very well.

As for statistics, again, all those functions are discussed there in the manual. Just realize that they're available––for things such as linear fits, weighted and moving averages, correlations, etc.

And be careful: Anytime you press [Σ+] or [Σ−], you're changing the contents of Registers 1 through 6. Don't clobber other important values you've stored there.

APPENDIX III. Bonds

Since you're comfortable with cash–flow diagrams, bonds (as the HP–12C sees them) are very easy to picture:

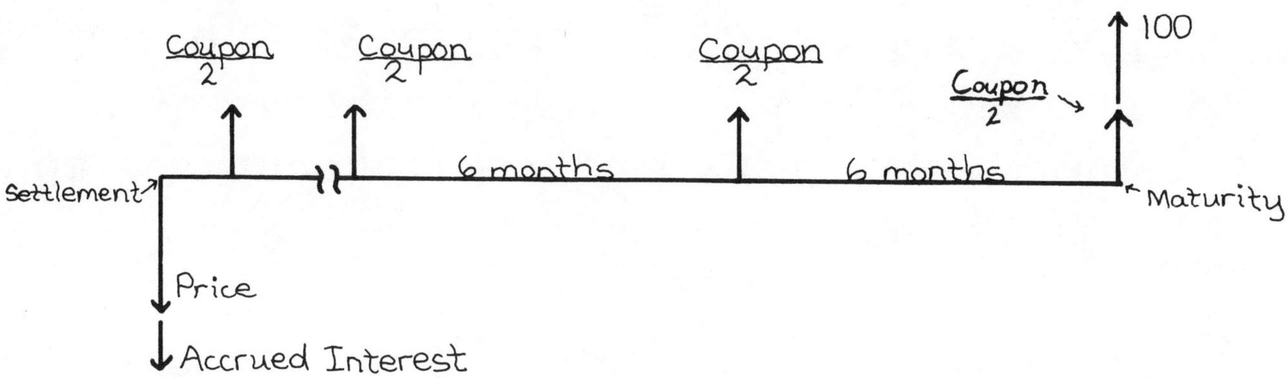

Notice these things:

1. The price you sell the bond for at "maturity" is always 100. This is called the "par" value. As far as the HP–12C's [YTM] and [PRICE] keys are concerned, you never sell before maturity, nor at a par value other than 100.

2. The "coupon" period is ALWAYS 6 months (semiannual). Therefore, the quoted dividend rate (often just called the "coupon")––which is always annualized and based upon a par value of 100–– represents TWICE the dividend you'll receive every 6 months.

3. The price you pay to the seller--on the "settlement date"--is increased by the amount of interest dividends due to the seller for the portion of the current coupon period for which the seller owned the bond. So the [PRICE] key gives you both quantities--the bid price in the X-register and the accrued interest in the Y-register.

4. The HP-12C always uses a 365-day "actual days" calendar to figure out the accrued interest (i.e., to count the days between the settlement date and the most recent coupon date).

SO BEWARE!

If you have any bond other than a 100-par-value, semi-annual-coupon, actual-days-basis bond, you CANNOT simply use the [PRICE] and [YTM] keys and expect the right answer.

What can you do...?

APPENDIX IV. Programming

You hear all this about non–integer n, two–part solutions you have to do yourself, bonds that don't fit, ACRS that isn't always a formula but sometimes is...Good grief...!

Do you just have to grit your teeth and crunch out all this stuff, one calculation at a time?

No Way!

That's what programming is all about. There's a whole facet of the HP–12C we haven't even mentioned yet.

To begin with, you need another picture of the "insides" of the HP–12C. Here's what program memory looks like:

You can have up to 99 steps in a program.

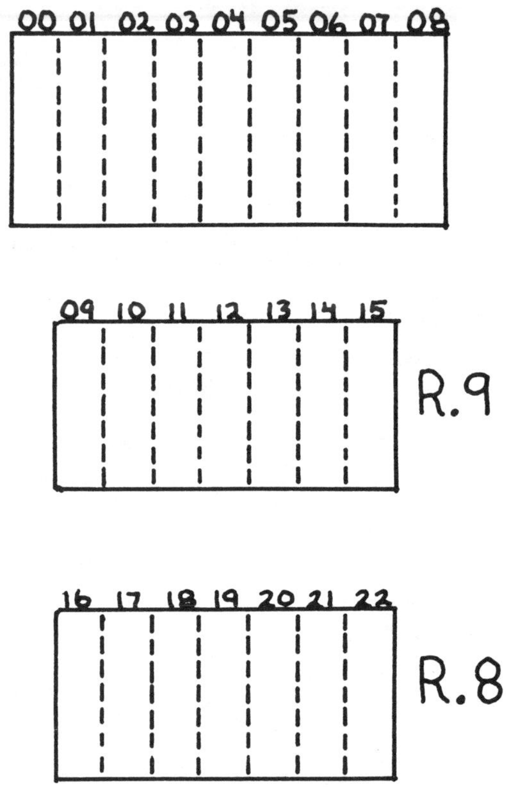

You get the first 8 program steps for free (00 is the first step, but step 01 is the first one you can use).

Then you start stealing the numbered storage registers—— one for every seven program steps——starting with R.9 and counting down.

If you put in a 99–step program, the only registers you'll be left with at the end are R0 through R6.

And, notice that once you use just one program step in a new register, that whole register is then off limits for storing numbers (STO 7, STO 8, etc.).

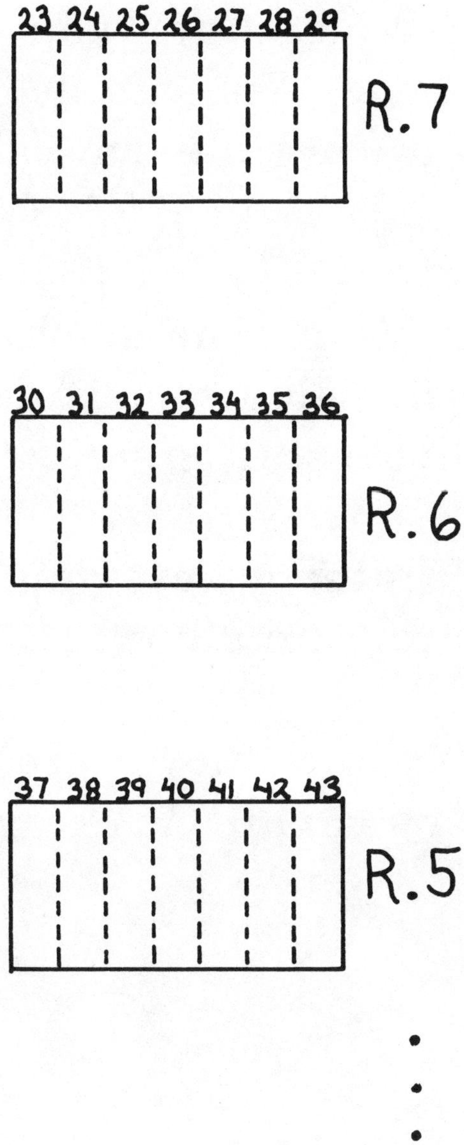

So how do you get at these program steps, anyway?

Simple. When you turn the calculator on, it's in RUN mode. You can do arithmetic, store numbers, and do all the financial calculations, etc.

Press [f] [P/R]. (P/R stands for "Program/Run." It switches the machine from one mode to the other.) The calculator is now in Program mode. See the little status indicator "PRGM" in the display?

Whatever keys you now press will be recorded as program steps.

If you've never programmed before, you may want to try this little program to multiply a number by 0.45:

While you're in program mode, and 00– is showing in the display, press these keys:

[.] [4] [5]

[X]

[g] [GTO] [0] [0].

Then get out of program mode (press [f] [P/R]),

and press: 1 [R/S].

The result is 0.45 (1 X 0.45 = 0.45).

Try pressing 2 [R/S], 3 [R/S]. etc. The program works!

Now, get back into PRGM mode (press [f] [P/R]).

If you only want to look at the steps already there--without changing any--you can move forward through the list of steps by using the [SST] (single–step forward) and [BST] (back–step) keys. Both of these operations are on the same key (with BST you press [g] first).

There's no "erase" key on the HP–12C. If you want to get rid of a certain step in a program you have to replace it with another (you just key the new one in right over the old one).

But, what do those numbers mean in the display? How do they represent program steps?

The two digits on the left represent the number of the step in the program (as you probably figured out). The other numbers are called "key–codes." Each pair of digits signifies a key on the keyboard by its position: row/column.

[X<>Y] is keycode 34 (row 3, column 4). [CHS] is 16. [X] is 20 (row 2, column 10 is called column 0). Etc.

The only exceptions to these are the digit keys. They are named by the numbers they represent.

For example:

[RCL] 5 is keycode 45 5. [STO] [PV] is 44 13.

[g] [BEG] is 43 7. It's pretty simple.

Of course, this notation isn't the most convenient in the world, but it's not bad, considering that the display can't form letters to spell the operations.

You already saw that when you want to switch back to RUN mode, you just press [f] [P/R] again. That one operation switches you back and forth between the two modes.

Now notice the CLEAR [PRGM] key. Pressing [f] [PRGM] will erase all program steps, but ONLY if you press it while in PRGM mode!

That's to prevent a fumble–fingered accident from wiping out a hard–fought program while you're just doing arithmetic or something else in RUN mode.

Remember! If you need to erase a program to reclaim some registers for storage, you can only use [f] [PRGM] while in PRGM mode!

As you've probably noticed, to help you out, there are a number of programs already written in the manual.

Sections 12 through 16 contain programs that are not only useful as applications (different sorts of bonds, leases, etc.) but they're a real help in practicing keying in programs and providing examples of working programs for you to study and pick apart.

But, don't rush right into them. First, work through the following example, and then take your time with sections 8 through 11 in the manual. REMEMBER, just as investments are money–earners only after you first spend money, programs are time–savers only after you first spend time.

Here's a good first example to start with if you want to learn how to program:

Write a program that will confirm both your checkbook and the monthly bank statement regarding your checking account. The program should do the following:

(1) Produce the same ending balance as your bank statement, given the same starting balance, all recorded deposits, cancelled checks and applied service charges.

(2) Produce your checkbook's current balance, given all other outstanding checks and deposits to date.

OK, look at that description for a minute.
It really describes:

(1) The results you want--the ANSWERS. In this case, they're the ending and current balances. These are the desired OUTPUTS.

(2) The things you already know--the things YOU tell the machine so it can solve the problem. These are the INPUTS.

So how do you start putting this into program form for the HP–12C?

One good way is to picture yourself when you're trying to use the program:

"Once the program is recorded in the calculator, how will I use it? What will I do first?"

(1) "I'll turn on the calculator." (This helps.)
(2) "I'll key in what I know—the INPUTS."
(3) Then I'll press some key that tells the HP–12C to give me the answers."

That sounds pretty trivial, and it will be, but first you'd better look more closely at those inputs. How many will there be? Are you going to have to store them all in registers? In what order will you key them in?

Of course, you can't predict just how many inputs there will be. One month you might have 10 checks and 2 deposits, but next month might involve 50 checks and 30 deposits. Obviously, you can't expect to store them all in the calculator--it only has about 30 registers all told. So that means you'll have to write the program so that it will use each input as you key it in, right?

For example, picture this as your procedure for running the program:

PART 1:
You key in -- the starting balance
-- the fixed monthly service charge
-- the per-check service charge

PART 2:
You press a key that will signify that you've completed part 1.

PART 3:
You key in either a deposit or a check.

PART 4:
You press a key to signify that you've completed part 3.

PART 5:
You repeat parts 3 and 4 until you've input all cancelled checks and recorded deposits.

PART 6:
The result in the display should agree with the bank's ending balance.

PART 7:
Now you repeat steps 3 and 4 until you've input all outstanding checks and deposits to date.

PART 8: The result in the display should agree with your checkbook.

Well, that sounds workable. Now, how are you going to tell the HP–12C that this is what you want to do?

ABOVE ALL, remember this: A program is little more than a recorded version of the keys you would otherwise press with your fingers.

Look, for example, at that little program back a few pages:

```
01  .
02  4
03  5
04  X
05  GTO 00
```

With this program recorded in the machine, you just keyed in a number and pressed [R/S] ("Run/Stop") to tell it that you're ready for it to "do its thing"––and it did. It multiplied what was in the X–register by .45.

Now what would you do if you had some number in the X–register, and you wanted to multiply it by .45?

Answer: You would press [.] [4] [5] [X]

Look familiar?

The only difference between the "manual" and "automatic" methods is that with the "automatic" program, you press [R/S] to tell it to run.

Now apply this to that 8–part procedure we just developed for the checkbook program:

PART 1: You key in the initial inputs.

Key in the starting balance and press ENTER.
Key in the fixed monthly service charge and press ENTER.
Key in the per–check service charge.
(If the service charges are zero, key in zeroes.)

PART 2: Now those three numbers are in the stack registers X, Y and Z. You press a key to tell the program to start running: R/S

(THE PROGRAM DOES SOMETHING HERE.)

PART 3: The program stops to let you key in either a recorded deposit amount or a cancelled check amount. Naturally, if it's a deposit, you key it in as a positive number; if it's a check, you key it in as negative (using the CHS key).

PART 4: You press R/S to tell the program to continue, since you're finished with this input.

(THE PROGRAM DOES SOMETHING HERE)

PART 5: You repeat what you did in parts 3 and 4--and so does the calculator--for each cancelled check or recorded deposit.

PART 6: You see the monthly ending balance in the display.

PART 7: Now you start repeating parts 3 and 4 again, except that this time, you just input all other outstanding checks and deposits (again, positive for deposits and negative for checks). The program repeats those parts, too.

PART 8: You see the current balance (to date) in the display.

(THE PROGRAM STOPS HERE)

You see how you gradually embellish each part as you envision more and more detail?

"O.K., but when do we write the actual program steps, anyway?"

Right now....

Here's the nice part: The only steps the program has to do are those in the parentheses after parts 2 and 4 (where it says, "THE PROGRAM DOES SOMETHING HERE")!

When you press [R/S] at PART 2, the stack looks like this:

T	?
Z	Starting balance for the month
Y	Fixed monthly service charge
X	Per–check service charge

What should happen? Well, you're going to want to keep a running total in the X–register so you can check this against the bank and your own checkbook. So the starting balance doesn't need to be stored anywhere else, but that per–check service charge does. So here are the first 4 steps of the program:

```
01   STO 0
02   R↓
03   –
04   R/S
```

Now the per–check charge amount is stored in register 0, and the balance in the X–register is the starting balance minus this month's fixed service charge. Notice how the program's correct operation depends upon the assumption that the inputs are keyed in in the same order every time.

Then at step 04, the program stops. (R/S in a program always means "STOP;" on the other hand, when you press [R/S] by hand, you usually mean "RUN.")

When the program stops, you then perform PART 3 of your procedure and press [R/S] (PART 4).

Now the program starts again. Because you've just keyed in a check or a deposit amount, the program has to figure out which one it was. After all, each check has a service charge associated with it--and this needs to be added to it--but deposits have no such charges:

```
05  0
06  X≤Y
07  GTO 12
08  R↓
09  RCL 0
10  −
11  ENTER
12  R↓
13  +
14  GTO 04
```

What's happening here?
You can see that the program then "keys in" a 0 underneath your input amount. Then at step 06, it asks a question: "Is the 0 in the X–register less than or equal to the amount (your check or deposit) in the Y–register?" If the answer is "yes," the program will continue at the next step. But if the answer is "no," the program will continue at step 08, skipping step 07. That's how these "question" steps work, and that's how programs make decisions.

In this case, if 0 is less than or equal to the input amount, that amount must be positive (a deposit) and so the program will do step 07, which merely tells it to skip to step 12. But if the amount is negative––for a check––steps 08–11 are performed.

These steps recall the per–check charge from register 0, add it to the check amount (subtracting because the amount is negative), and then finally, at step 13, this amount is added to the running total.

Of course, that final addition at step 13 is all that gets done in the case of a deposit. See if you can tell why the R↓'s and ENTER are necessary here. It may help to draw stack diagrams for this program.

Finally––in either case––the last step just sends the program back to step 04, which tells it to stop so you can input the next amount.

Here's the whole program, the keystrokes you would use to record the program steps, and the steps as they appear in the display:

STEPS		KEYSTROKES	DISPLAY	
00		[f] [P/R]	00–	
		[f] CLEAR [PRGM]	00–	
01	STO 0	[STO] 0	01–	44 0
02	R↓	[R↓]	02–	33
03	–	[–]	03–	30
04	R/S	[R/S]	04–	31
05	0	0	05–	0
06	X≤Y	[g] [X≤Y]	06–	43 34
07	GTO 12	[g] [GTO] 12	07–	43, 33 12
08	R↓	[R↓]	08–	33
09	RCL 0	[RCL] 0	09–	45 0
10	–	[–]	10–	30
11	ENTER	[ENTER]	11–	36
12	R↓	[R↓]	12–	33
13	+	[+]	13–	40
14	GTO 04	[g] [GTO] 04	14–	43, 33 04

[f] [P/R] (Normal numerical display)

Notice that before you begin to key in the steps, you should clear out any other program steps that may be lurking in program memory. That's what that [f] CLEAR [PRGM] step is all about.

So go ahead and try this program with your latest bank statement!

QUESTION: After you've used the program once, how do you tell the calculator to start back at step 01 again? Otherwise, it will just keep on repeating steps 04 through 12, right?

Right. To tell it to start the program from the beginning again, just press:

[g] [GTO] 00

Be sure to do this when the calculator is in RUN mode-- NOT in PRGM mode.

What this does is to reposition the program "pointer"--the thing that tells the machine what step it's ON--back to step 00, where it's ready for you to press [R/S] after you do PARTS 1 & 2 of your procedure.

So, those are the ground rules and some good starting examples.

But that certainly doesn't even begin to cover the subject of programming itself. That would take at least another book. The best advice to you at this point is to study sections 8 through 11 in the manual, slowly and patiently.

As you know, the whole premise of this book has been that you can learn the basics of financial problem–solving, with a small investment of time.

Well, it takes a lot bigger investment of time to learn to program well. You can't cheat it––you have to pay the price. Go easy––go slowly.

APPENDIX V.
Tidbits and Handy Hints
[12x] and [12÷]

You're probably wondering why we never used the [12x] and [12÷] keys in our keystroke solutions. There are two reasons:

1. The more practice you get in using arithmetic in the stack, the better.

2. It's too easy to get in the habit of using these keys when they don't apply––when you're first learning. As you become a financial wizard, you'll find these operations convenient for problems with monthly D.I.P.'s. But remember, they're dangerously useless for daily, weekly, quarterly, or yearly D.I.P.'s!

Enough said. For a brief description of these operations, see your manual (in the key index).

CONFIRMING AN A.P.R.

Sometimes you may have trouble confirming the interest rate quoted by a bank. The probable reason for this is that banks often use a 365/360 day basis for daily compounding. This means that the nominal A.P.R. is divided by 360 to get the daily D.I.R. But the compounding year used is 365 days long. So to compute the effective yearly rate, you would compound that D.I.R. for 365 days (n = 365).

BONDS WITH PAR VALUE OTHER THAN 100

Here's a nice thing to know if you're ever faced with a bond that's just right for the HP–12C except it has a par value (a resale price) other than 100.

To compute a correct Yield, given quotes for Coupon, Par Value, Price, and Accrued Interest (A.I.):

Use (100/Par Value) X Quoted Coupon as your actual Coupon rate;

Use (100/Par Value) X (Quoted Price + Quoted A.I.) as your actual (Price + A.I).

To compute a correct Price and A.I., given quotes for Par Value, Yield and Coupon:

Using (100/ParValue) X Quoted Coupon as the actual Coupon, compute the Price and A.I., and multiply the resulting numbers by (Par Value/100).

This makes for a handy program to write. eh?

LINEAR REGRESSION

If you're trying to fit a straight line to some data pairs (X1,Y1), (X2,Y2), etc., what you really want to know is the equation of the line:

$$Y = mX + b.$$

You can find the slope, m, and the Y–intercept, b, by doing the following:

Key in the data pairs like this: [f] [Σ], Y1 [ENTER] X1 [Σ+], Y2 [ENTER] X2 [Σ+], etc., until you've keyed in all you're data pairs (you need at least 2 pairs to fit a straight line to them).

0 [g] [y,r] gives you the Y–intercept, b.

[STO] 0 stores b temporarily.

1 [g] [y,r]
[RCL] [0] [–] gives you the slope, m.

Again, it makes for a good program to write (hint, hint...).

NO SOLUTION TO IRR

What do you do when there's no solution or more than one solution to IRR?

The first thing you should do is read Appendix B in the Owner's Handbook.

If you've exhausted all those possibilities and still haven't come up with a number that can be called a yield, you could try getting a Modified Internal Rate of Return (MIRR).

Here's a cash–flow situation for which there are probably multiple IRR's:

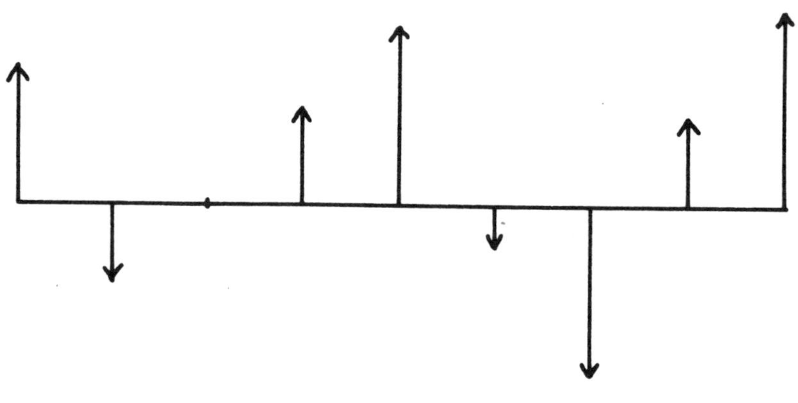

Before you can compute an MIRR, you have to know two other numbers: the "safe rate" and the "risk rate."

The "safe rate" is the highest rate you know that you can earn in a secured liquid account.

The "risk rate" is the highest rate you can invest at--during the time represented on the diagram--and reasonably expect to be able to liquidate at the end of that interval.

The procedure is this:

1. You discount (slide back) all of the negative cash-flows at the safe rate. Use NPV to do this with the safe rate in the i-register (don't forget to match it to the D.I.P.).

2. You slide forward, to the far (future) end, all of your positive cash-flows, using the risk rate (remember how to compute a Net Future Value? Page 174).

3. Now, with just one cash-flow at either end of the time line, use the 5-key solution to compute what periodic rate that represents. That's your MIRR.

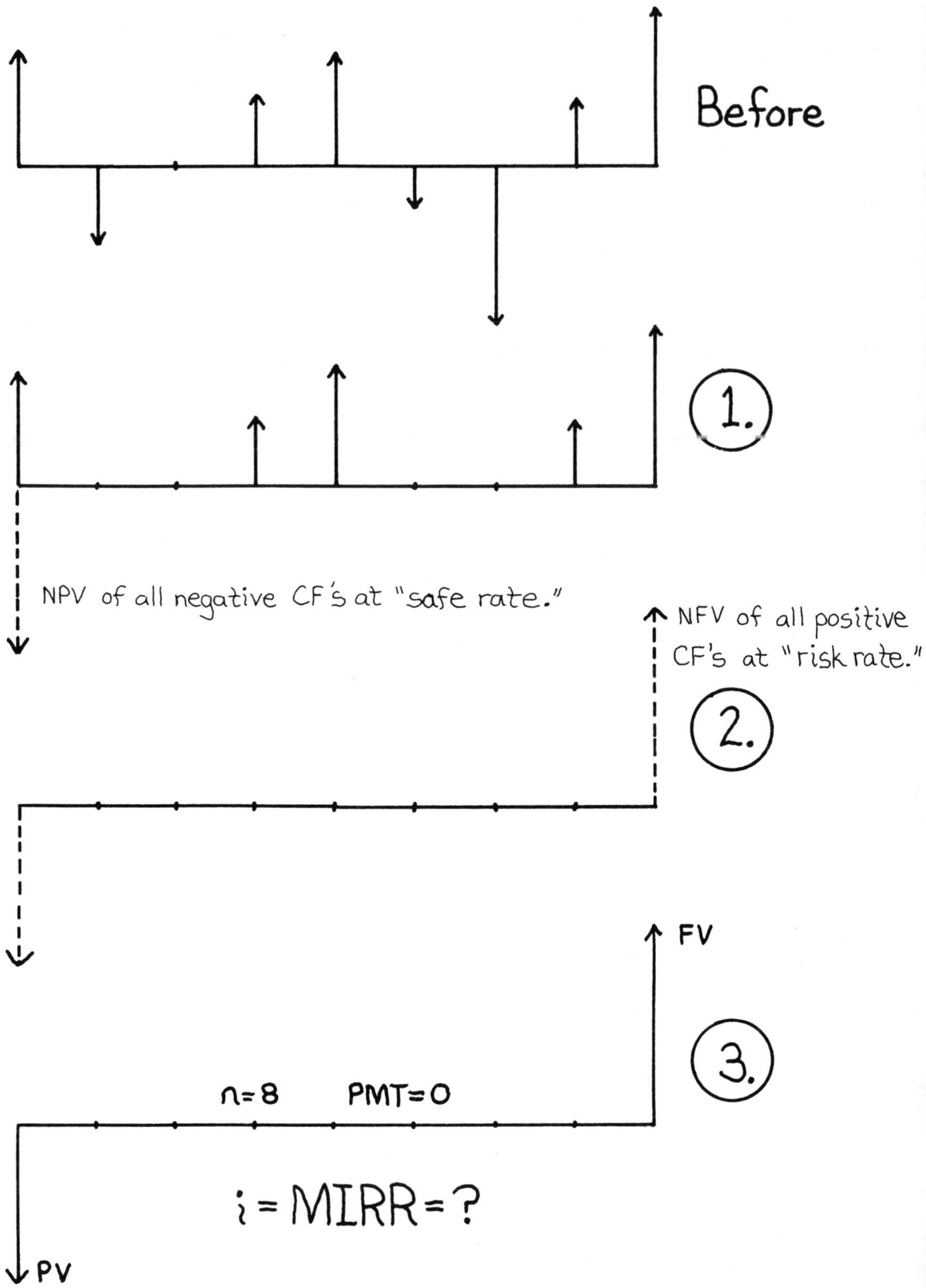
Before
1.
NPV of all negative CF's at "safe rate."
NFV of all positive CF's at "risk rate."
2.
FV
3.
n=8 PMT=0
i = MIRR = ?
PV

What you're doing here is really quite simple: You're using the old slide–and–shrink rule to simplify things.

You know you're only going to invest what you have to, but you want to be sure the money's there when you need to invest it. So you ask, "What's the amount I have to salt away now in a safe, liquid account, so that when the times come for these outlays of cash, I'll have just enough?" The answer is given to you by the NPV of your negative cash–flows, using the safe rate as the discount rate.

On the other end, you know that every time you get a cash–flow back, you're going to let it ride in a high–yield market of some kind––put some icing on the cake, so to speak––until the end of the analysis period. "So," you ask, "what's the most all these reinvested returns will add up to at the end?" Your answer is the NFV of those returns, computed with that high–yield "risk–rate."

There you go––the minimum money you need up front the maximum money you can get out of it at the end. Find the yield on that simple, one–shot investment/return, and that's a pretty good analysis of that whole "BEFORE" mess. (Slide–and–shrink strikes again!)

APPENDIX VI. One–Minute Mysteries: Errors and Other Weird Behavior

There will be times when your calculator appears to be rebelling. You should get in the habit of looking in Appendix C in the case of ERROR messages and in the index for other problems, but here are a few of the stranger ones.

1. SYMPTOM

A comma has replaced the decimal point in the display.

EXPLANATION

This is European notation.

CURE

Turn the calculator off; press and HOLD DOWN the [.] key; turn on the machine while holding down the [.] key (you'll see no display), release the [.] key. (Of course if you're European, this will also correct that strange American notation.)

2. SYMPTOM

The display has two numbers at the far right, and the results aren't making any sense. The display looks something like this: 1.234567 89.

EXPLANATION

This is the scientific notation display format. You get this by pressing [f] [.] (see the manual.)

CURE

Just press [f] [2], or [f] [4], or whatever number of decimal places you want to see.

3. SYMPTOM

Pressing [g] [s] gives you ERROR 2, and you're sure that none of the causes in Appendix C (in the manual) are to blame.

EXPLANATION

You've probably been using [Σ+] to accumulate some X–values––without paying attention to what's in the Y–register.

Under some circumstances, the number in the Y–register can cause

$$\frac{n\Sigma y^2 - (\Sigma y)^2}{n(n-1)}$$

to be less than zero, which causes an ERROR.

The ERROR has nothing to do with your X–data. (Remember: [s] always finds the standard deviation of both accumulated X–data and accumulated Y–data.)

CURE

Before you begin to key in all your X–values, just press 0 [ENTER], or [f] [Σ] (clears registers 1 through 6 and the stack).

4. SYMPTOM

ERROR 4 is telling you that some of your registers aren't there––say, all registers beyond R8, for example. But you already pressed [f] [PRGM] to clear out any program steps that could have swiped those registers.

EXPLANATION

Ah, but did you press [f] [PRGM] while the HP–12C was in Program Mode?!?

[f] [PRGM] will only clear those program steps away when in program mode.

CURE

[f] [P/R] [f] [PRGM] [f] [P/R].

Now all 20 numbered registers are available.

5. SYMPTOM

ERROR 5 is staring you in the face. You know you're doing something wrong in a 5–key calculation, but what?

EXPLANATION

Most likely, it's one of two things:
1. Did you violate the cash–flow sign conventions?
2. Did you give it a problem that has no solution?

CURE

The first one is easy to correct. Look at the second one:

For example, if you give the calculator a loan with $300 payments, but the interest alone will amount to over $300, you'll never pay off that loan. In fact, the balance will grow––not shrink. And if you ask the HP–12C how many months it will take to pay off this loan, it will just laugh at you––in the form of ERROR 5.

6. SYMPTOM

ERROR 8 comes up when you try to do some bond calculation. You're sure that you have M.DY or D.MY correctly set.

EXPLANATION

You've input a maturity date on a day of the month that has no corresponding day in the coupon month (six months prior).

Examples:

December 31	(No June 31)
March 31	(No September 31)
May 31	(No November 31)
August 29, 30, 31	(No February 29,30,31, usually)
October 31	(No April 31)

The calculator works on an actual days basis, so the coupon date it's looking for is the same day of the month as the maturity date. If that's an erroneous day for the coupon month, the calculator just throws in the towel.

CURE

For all cases except August 29th and 30th, just shift all dates forward one day. For August 29th and 30th--who knows? There's no single accepted method in the securities industry for handling these dates.

APPENDIX VII: USING THIS COURSE WITH OTHER CALCULATORS

As you'll see, most of this book is a course in problem–solving, and these methods certainly aren't limited to the HP–12C. So if you own an HP–37, HP–38, HP–67/97*, or HP–41*, large portions of this book are directly applicable to your machine(s), too.

Of course, since each model is different, the sections explaining the keyboard and storage registers aren't pertinent, and you'll need to read in your owner's manual for those details. A complete list of recommended pages will follow.

The main thing to keep in mind at this point is that in the sections on problem–solving, the METHOD is important (i.e., how to think about and set up the problem, what to solve for first, etc.), but the KEYSTROKES will, of course, vary with the model of calculator you have.

*(with either of the applicable HP software pacs: "FINANCIAL DECISIONS" or "REAL ESTATE.")

Here's a recommended course outline:

IF YOU HAVE AN HP–37:

Pages 16–57 and pages 60–145 will pretty well cover the fundamentals of your calculator's capabilities.

IF YOU HAVE AN HP–38:

You're in luck; the whole book is quite relevant, except for the appendices (yet even the programming appendix is applicable). This is not a coincidence; the HP–38 and the HP–12C are very closely related, and therefore even their few differences are important for you to understand. They have the same memory capacities, most of the same keys and keystrokes. So go back to page 7 and plow on ahead.

IF YOU HAVE AN HP–67/97 OR AN HP–41*:

Start on page 74 and read straight through page 204. AND KEEP IN MIND: you're after the concepts involved. The appropriate keystrokes are outlined in the software pac you're using.

*(with either of the applicable HP software pacs: "FINANCIAL DECISIONS" or "REAL ESTATE.")

We hope you get a lot out of this book, that it is both accessible and memorable, and that it will continue to be so in the future, whenever you need a refresher course.

We believe this simple, conversational format is the best for quick, high-retention learning. We've tried to simulate on paper the kind of conversation you would hear in a classroom--just one human being talking with another.

And because we're just human beings (how did you like that lead-in?), there may be plottographical errors, or discussions that could be clearer, or (heaven forbid) numerical errors. If you find any, please let us know so we can keep improving the course. Thanks for listening, and may your calculator show you...

MANY HAPPY RETURN$

February 1984

TABLE OF CONTENTS

CONTENTS PAGE

CONTENTS PAGE

Other Books Also Available From The Press At GRAPEVINE PUBLICATIONS, INC.

—*An Easy Course in Programming the HP-41*

—*Using Your HP-41 Advantage ROM: Statics for Students*

—*Using Your HP-41 Advantage ROM: Electrical Circuits for Students*

—*Computer Science On Your HP-41 (using the Advantage ROM)*

—*An Easy Course in Programming the HP-11C and HP-15C*

—*The HP-16C Training Guide*

—*An Easy Course in Using the HP-12C and Other HP Financial Calculators*

—*The HP-12C Pocket Guide: Just In Case*

—*The HP Business Consultant Training Guide*

—*The HP Business Consultant Pocket Companion*

Books from Grapevine make *perfect* gifts... on every occasion!

(Please see next page for order blank.)

BOOKS & THEIR PRICES

An Easy Course in Programming the HP-41	$19.95
Using Your HP-41 Advantage ROM: Statics for Students	$11.95
Using Your HP-41 Advantage ROM: Electrical Circuits for Students	$11.95
Computer Science On Your HP-41 (using the Advantage ROM)	$14.95
An Easy Course in Programming the HP-11C and HP-15C	$19.95
The HP-16C Training Guide	$24.95
An Easy Course in Using the HP-12C and Other HP Financial Calculators	$19.95
The HP-12C Pocket Guide: Just In Case	$4.95
The HP Business Consultant Training Guide	$21.95
The HP Business Consultant Pocket Companion	$7.95

SHIPPING & HANDLING

Surface Post (allow 2-3 weeks): $2.00
UPS (for faster delivery): $3.50

Please check with your nearest Hewlett-Packard Dealer to save time & shipping costs!
(Prices subject to change without notice.)

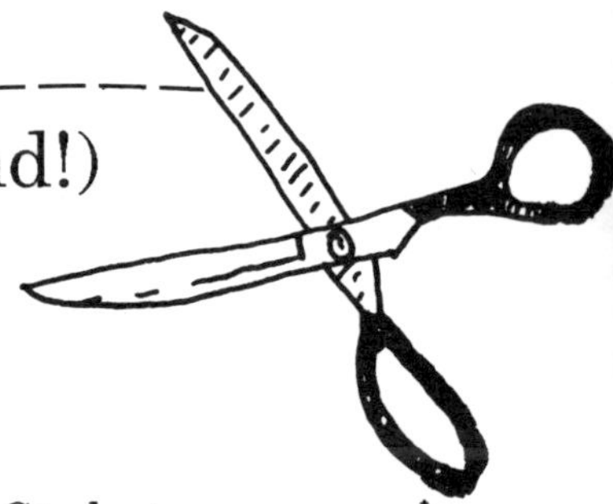

ORDER FORM (Impress A Friend!)

Please send me:

__ Copies of *An Easy Course in Programming the HP-41*
__ Copies of *Using Your HP-41 Advantage ROM: Statics for Students*
__ Copies of *Using Your HP-41 Advantage ROM: Electrical Circuits for Students*
__ Copies of *Computer Science On Your HP-41 (using the Advantage ROM)*
__ Copies of *An Easy Course in Programming the HP-11C and HP-15C*
__ Copies of *The HP-16C Training Guide*
__ Copies of *An Easy Course in Using the HP-12C and Other HP Financial Calculators*
__ Copies of *The HP-12C Pocket Guide: Just In Case*
__ Copies of *The HP Business Consultant Training Guide*
__ Copies of *The HP Business Consultant Pocket Companion*

__Check Enclosed __MasterCard __VISA Signature__________________________

Account No.______________________________Expiration Date__________

Ship My Books To:

NAME______________________________

ADDRESS______________________________

CITY______________STATE___ZIP________

TELEPHONE______________________________

AMOUNT OF PAYMENT:

Cost of Books________
Shipping Cost________
TOTAL ________

Make cheques payable and send to:

Grapevine Publications, Inc.
P.O. Box 118
Corvallis, OR 97339-0118, U.S.A.

Or call our Toll-Free "Order Line:" 1-800-338-4331

THANK YOU!